Computing for Psychologists

Computing for Psychologists

Statistical Analysis Using SPSS and MINITAB

By

Robert West
Royal Holloway and Bedford New College
University of London

hơ
ap harwood academic publishers
chur · london · paris · new york · melbourne

10

Harwood Academic Publishers

Post Office Box 197
London WC2E 9PX
United Kingdom

58, rue Lhomond
75005 Paris
France

Post Office Box 786
Cooper Station
New York, New York 10276
United States of America

Private Bag 8
Camberwell, Victoria 3124
Australia

Library of Congress Cataloging-in-Publication Data

West, Robert, 1955-
    Computing for psychologists : statistical analysis using SPSS and
MINITAB / Robert West.
        p. cm.
    Includes index.
    ISBN 3-7186-5085-1 (hard). -- ISBN 3-7186-5086-X (soft)
    1. Psychology--Statistical methods--Data processing. 2. SPSS
(Computer program) 3. Minitab (Computer system) 4. Psychology
--Data processing. I. Title.
BF39.W45   1990
519.5'0285'536--dc20   90-5391
                                                                  CIP

Dedication

To Matthew, Jamie and Daniel.

Acknowledgements

I would like to thank my wife Anne, Davina French, Peter Howell and Donald McBurney for helpful comments on various drafts.

Contents

Preface

My original intention for this book was for one which covered both analysis of data and programming for experiments. The former was to be treated by providing a guide to one or more statistical packages; the latter was to be a guide to programming in an appropriate computer language. Both of these aspects of computing are taught to undergraduates at Royal Holloway and Bedford New College, University of London where I work. Market research soon made it clear, however, that programming is not widely taught to psychology students and where it is taught the languages used and the approaches adopted vary greatly. Therefore, a practical guide to programming which would have to be based on one language would have a small readership, whatever language was chosen. There was more consensus about the use of ready-made statistics programs for analysing data and so this book focuses on that aspect of psychological computing. My aim has been to keep it short, affordable and to the point. Instead of wading through impenetrable manuals, the reader should be able to look up what statistical function he or she wishes to perform and find a ready-made template specifically geared towards his or her needs as a psychologist or psychology student.

Introduction

I.1 About this book

This is a course-book and reference book for psychologists and Psychology students wanting to use computers to carry out their statistical analyses.

Most computer-based statistical analysis in Psychology is carried out by using pre-existing computer programs, otherwise known as **statistical packages**. There are quite a few statistical packages. This book focuses exclusively on two of these. One is called **SPSS** which stands for **Statistical Package for the Social Sciences** and the other is called **MINITAB.**

This book can be used to accompany a statistics course in which the **statistical analyses** and the **means to carry them out** using a computer are taught together. It will not be the main statistics text. Instead it will enable the statistical procedures described in course notes or statistics texts to be implemented on computer.

It covers most of the statistical analyses taught at undergraduate level and some analyses that are usually taught at graduate level. Thus it should see students through most of their university training.

The book can also be used by academic psychologists and clinicians who have already undergone their statistical training but now need to know how to carry out their analyses using SPSS or MINITAB.

There are already a large number of statistics books on the market and many of these mention how to carry out analyses using one or more statistical packages. Unfortunately these books do not give enough attention to the things that novices need to know to enable them to work the statistical packages. For example, they do not describe how to operate computers, how to enter data into computers and how to interact with the computer effectively.

This book aims to fill this gap. It assumes no prior knowledge of computers and as far as possible it covers everything that one needs to know to carry out statistical analysis using the two packages under consideration. It takes the reader step by step through the processes of data entry and data analysis.

There are many different kinds of computer each of which has to be operated slightly differently. The commands that have to be typed in to carry out analyses using SPSS and MINITAB are almost exactly the same regardless of which computer one is working on. However, the commands that one uses to enter data into the computer, save it and generally interact with the computer do differ from one kind of computer to the other. It is not possible in this book to describe how to work all the various computers that might be used. Therefore this book has focused on two of the most popular.

If you are using SPSS or MINITAB on a mainframe computer known as a **VAX** which uses an operating system known as **VMS,** then this book should tell you everything you need to know. You can easily check with your college's computer centre or your department's computer representative to see if this is the case. The question to ask is: "Do we have a VAX running VMS?"

If you are using SPSS or MINITAB on an **IBM PC, AT, XT, 386,** or **486** microcomputer which uses an operating system known as **MSDOS,** then this book contains all the information you need to know. In fact, if you have any computer that has MSDOS as its operating system, then this book has all you need to know. As a member of staff, you might have one of these desktop computers in your office. As a student there may be a room in the department that has several of these computers available for general use. The question you need to ask is: "Do we have any IBM or IBM clone microcomputers running MSDOS?"

Do not be concerned if the terminology in the last two paragraphs seemed obscure to you. It is explained in Chapter 1. It is raised here only to enable you to assess how useful this book is likely to be to you.

If you have access to a computer that does not fall into either of the above categories, this book should still serve as a useful course-book and reference. However, you will need to get some additional information about how to operate your particular computer from the computer centre or your department's computer representative. This will probably take the form of a short hand-out of a dozen or so pages.

I.2 Coverage

SPSS and MINITAB have an extensive range of features. To cover them all would require a very weighty volume indeed. I have decided to keep this book short partly to keep the price down and partly to avoid overloading the reader. Many of the facilities available within these packages are in any event of little or no interest to psychologists. This book is a primer, designed to get you into the packages concerned and show you how to perform standard analyses.

There are two ways in which you can extend your knowledge of SPSS and MINITAB once you have finished this book. You can use the **help facilities** that they provide to explore the various options. Use of these facilities is described in this book. Alternatively, you can seek advice from an expert or even read the manuals!

In the case of the multivariate statistics and analysis of variance procedures described in Chapter 8 onwards I can strongly recommend that you read "Using Multivariate Statistics (2nd Ed.)" by B. G. Tabachnick and L. S. Fidell. Cambridge, Harper and Row, 1989. Besides describing the statistical analyses in a readable manner, this book provides commands to carry out these analyses using, amongst other programs, SPSS-X.

I.2 Misuse of statistical packages

One of the dangers of the ready availability of powerful statistical tools is that these will be used inappropriately or the results misinterpreted. Although this book is not a statistics manual, I felt it important to describe some of the main pitfalls associated with using some of the statistical procedures described. I also give a brief introduction to each of the statistical operations described, indicating when it is used and why. If you are using this book as part of, or in parallel with, a statistics course, this should help to reinforce the link between the statistics and the computing. If you are using this book having already learned about the statistical methods, it should just act as a refresher. You will notice that the statistical background provided for the multivariate procedures (Chapters 11 to 13) is greater than for the more basic undergraduate level statistics. This is because the options available on the computer are more extensive and informed choices need to be made about them.

Looking back over years of statistical computing and watching others making the same mistakes that I made has led me to include a few tips on making the best use of statistical packages. The amount of time and effort that can be wasted by adopting inefficient work practices is enormous. I hope I can save the reader some of this wasted time and effort.

I.3 Some words of warning

A couple of words of warning are in order. The first few weeks of learning to use a computer can be very frustrating. One often types in commands that look perfectly OK but they just do not work. The reason is often something very difficult to spot such as a punctuation mark missing or a space where there should not be one. It requires **perseverance** to get on the right tracks and a preparedness to keep trying things out. Eventually, however, a point is reached where it comes fairly easily and it is inconceivable that one would do even the most basic statistics by hand.

Another point you need to bear in mind is that books like this cannot be read as you would read a novel or Psychology textbook. In books on computing, **every word has to be read and understood**. You cannot afford to skip over parts. Inevitably, you will come to a point in trying out an example when you cannot proceed any further. This will involve you going back over ground you have already covered and re-reading the appropriate sections. Be prepared to look backwards and forwards through this book as necessary until you get the basic principles. After that it can be used simply for reference purposes.

I.4 Using this book

You should read Chapter 1; then, depending on what computer and statistical package you will be using, follow the instructions at the end of that chapter.

There are numerous examples dotted around this book. **You should try these examples out and make them work**. It is only by doing this that you will become proficient in the use of the statistics package concerned and build up your confidence. The back of the book contains Appendices with examples of complete sessions with the computer. You should try these out as well.

Happy computing!

Chapter 1

Some information about computers and an overview of SPSS and MINITAB

This chapter will describe the features common to nearly all computers and then go on to describe some of the more widely available types and makes. If you already know about computers, you can skip most of this chapter and go straight to Section 1.8.

By the time you finish this chapter you should know about the following:

- the main parts of computers, especially discs and disc drives
- how information is stored in a computer, especially what is meant by "byte", "kilobyte", "megabyte" and "ASCII"
- files and file names
- using the computer keyboard
- operating systems
- types of computer (specifically mainframes vs microcomputers)
- what you have to do in a typical session with SPSS or MINITAB

1.1 Computer hardware

The circuitry and electrical components of computers are known as **hardware**. Computer hardware generally consists of sets of **integrated circuits** (**ICs** or **chips**) made out of silicon, attached to a **printed circuit board** (**PCB**). The PCBs are connected together by a frame sometimes called a **backplane**.

ICs are made up of hundreds, thousands or even tens of thousands of tiny electrical components known as **transistors** etched into the silicon and joined together in complex circuits. They are about the size of a thumbnail and encased in plastic with pins sticking out for connecting the chip to the PCB. PCBs join these ICs together by strands of conducting metal printed on to the plastic of the board.

The CPU

At the heart of the computer is the **Central Processing Unit** (**CPU**). This is the part of the machine that carries out instructions such as moving information around, adding up numbers, comparing numbers and so on.

The bus

All the other parts of the computer are linked to the CPU and each other via a circuit known as a **bus**. Figure 1.1 shows schematically the various parts of a computer linked to the bus.

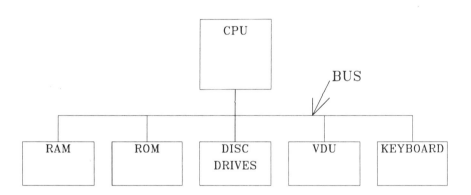

Figure 1.1 Schematic representation of main components in computers. See text for details.

Memory

Computers need to be able to hold information. This may be information in the form of a set of instructions to the CPU (a **program**), or information to be used by the CPU in executing those instructions (**data**). Linked via the bus to the CPU is the computer's electronic memory. There are two forms of memory: **Random Access Memory (RAM)**, and **Read Only Memory (ROM)**.

RAM is for temporary storage of programs and data while the computer is switched on. ROM is for permanent storage of important programs that the computer needs in order to be able to function (e.g. **operating systems** - see below).

Most of the computer's RAM is normally **volatile**. This means that the information it contains is lost when the power to the computer is switched off. Also this memory is not large enough to hold all the information that the computer is ever likely to need. Therefore most computers have permanent storage devices also attached to the bus.

Disc drives

The most commonly used permanent storage device is the **disc drive**. A disc drive is a device that stores information on computer discs and reads information from those discs. Computer discs are coated with magnetic material similar to that used on audio tapes. Information is written on to, and read from, the discs by a read/write head in the disc drive, again similar to the system for audio recording and playback.

The keyboard

Users need to be able to enter information or commands into the computer. This is normally done by means of a typewriter-style **keyboard**. Computer keyboards have many more keys than a typewriter. The extra keys perform special functions depending on the computer and the program it is running (see Figure 1.2).

The VDU

Users also need to be able to view the results (or **output**) of computer programs. Mostly this is done via a TV-style **monitor,** otherwise known as a **visual display unit (VDU).** VDUs are usually about 14 inches across and can display 24 or more lines each of 80 characters. VDUs can be either **monochrome** or **colour.**

Monochrome VDUs are generally either black on white, or amber or green on black. They can all display **text** (letters, numbers etc.). They may or may not be capable of displaying **graphics** (pictures, line drawings etc.). Colour VDUs can normally display both text and graphics. Both monochrome and colour VDUs vary in the **resolution** with which they can display text and graphics. Very high-resolution VDUs can display 1,000 or more **pixels** (little dots that make up the picture) across the screen. Low resolution VDUs may be able to display as few as 400.

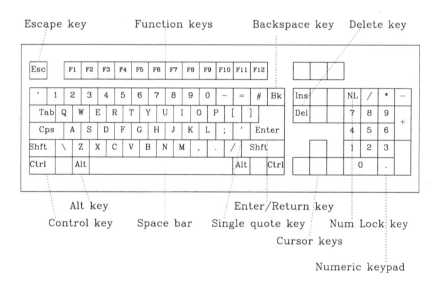

Figure 1.2 Representation of a typical computer keyboard. Some keyboards do not have the numeric keypad and the cursor keys may be in a different place but the basic layout is usually the same.

The printer

It is also possible to obtain a permanent record of the computer output by means of a **printer**. There are many different kinds of printer. **Line-printers** are very fast and expensive but the quality of output is relatively poor. **Daisy-wheel printers** work like automatic typewriters; the quality is good but they tend to be slow, and they are limited to printing text. **Dot-matrix printers** (e.g. the NEC P2200) use patterns of tiny pins to construct the shape of characters and then strike through a ribbon to make the imprint on the page. They vary enormously in speed and quality. However, even the less expensive ones produce quite good text and graphics output. Ones with 24 or 48 pins are generally better than ones with only 8 pins. **Ink-jet printers** (e.g. the Hewlett-Packard DeskJet) can produce fairly high quality text and graphics. They work by squirting ink at the page. **Laser printers** produce the highest quality text and graphics currently available. There are two kinds: **bit-mapped** and **postscript**. Bit-mapped laser printers (e.g. the Hewlett-Packard LaserJet) are relatively restricted in the range of type-faces and sizes that can be produced. Postscript laser printers (e.g. the Apple Laserwriter) have a vast range of type faces that are **scalable** to just about any size you wish. They are about twice the price of bit-mapped laser printers. The print in this book was produced by an Apple Laserwriter Plus.

1.2 In what form is information stored in computers?

Bits

Present day computers store information digitally; that is, in patterns of 1s and 0s. A single unit that can be either 1 or 0 is known as a **bit** (binary digit). A set of eight bits together can make up to 256 different configurations, for example:

```
00000000
00000001
00000010
00000011
```

Bytes

Sets of eight bits are known as **bytes**. A byte is normally used to represent one of three things:

a number

a character

a command to the CPU

If a single byte is used to represent a number it could represent integers between 0 and 255, or -127 to +127 with one of the bits being used to indicate whether the number is positive or negative.

Words

More usually bytes are strung together into **words** of two, four, six or eight bytes. In that case, special conventions are used that allow very large numbers and numbers with many decimal places to be represented by a word.

ASCII

When a byte is used to represent a character a convention has to be adopted to assign each character to each pattern of 1s and 0s. The most common code (and one that you will come across later) is known as **ASCII** (American Standard Code for Information Interchange). Here are some examples of bytes and their corresponding characters in ASCII:

Character	Byte
a	01100001
b	01100010
.	
.	
.	
A	01000001
B	01000010
.	
.	
1	00110001
2	00110010
.	

There are two things to notice: upper case letters (e.g. A) have different codes from lower case letters (e.g. a); digits are also represented.

The data you enter into the computer for analysis will be stored as ASCII characters. The statistics package you use will have to convert from the character format to a proper number format so that it can do the necessary maths.

Although I have given examples of ASCII code, you need not worry about which bytes correspond to which characters - the computer will take care of that for you. You just have to bear in mind that when you enter data into the computer it will normally be in the form of ASCII characters whereas the statistical package needs it in a special, numerical form - so a special **read in** operation needs to be performed when you analyze the data. More about that later.

The third kind of thing that bytes can represent is an instruction to the CPU. When certain bytes are sent to special locations in the CPU, the CPU carries out the corresponding instructions. You do not need to worry about this any more. I just mention it for the sake of completeness. Neither do you need to worry about how the computer knows when a byte is supposed to be a number, character or CPU instruction - this is taken care of by the computer itself.

1.3 Files and file names

Information on discs is stored as **files**. These can be thought of as like files in a filing cabinet. Each file has a unique **file name** that the person who created the file gives it. Here are some examples of file names that can be used with the types of computer you are likely to use:

EXAMPLE.DAT
REACTION.DAT
SURVEY.RES

You will notice that they consist of two parts, separated by a full stop. The first part, the **prefix**, can be up to eight characters long and should be used to indicate the subject matter of whatever is contained in the file. The second part, the **suffix**, should be up to three characters long, and should be used to indicate what kind of a file it is. Thus DAT might be used to remind you that it contains data; RES might be used to remind you that it contains a report of the results of your statistical analysis. There is more information on file names relevant to your specific requirements in Appendices 1 and 2 and in Chapters 2 and 4.

Everything you do centres on the use of files. The statistics packages are stored on disc as files as are the data on which you will perform the statistical operations.

1.4 Types of Computer

The main types of computers are:

Supercomputers
These are extremely fast computers, not necessarily all that large physically, but geared up towards high-speed "number crunching". They are used for weather forecasting, defence projects, sophisticated moving graphics, and large computer simulations (including simulations of psychological processes). Perhaps the most well-known supercomputer is the **Cray**. They are usually attached to conventional mainframes (see below) and can only be accessed via those mainframes. The mainframes act as a **front end** for the supercomputers.

Mainframes
Mainframes have large CPUs and masses of RAM, usually more than 100 million bytes (a million bytes is known as a **Megabyte** or **MB**). They also have large numbers of very fast discs with massive storage capacity (thousands of MB). The discs on mainframes are left in place permanently so that a user can gain access to his or her files at any time. Mainframes also have high speed line-printers that produce printed **output** or **hard copy**.

Mainframes serve the needs of hundreds of users at the same time. Each user sits at a **terminal** (VDU and keyboard). Terminals may be spread over a wide area linked to the main computer via cables, optical fibre links or telephone lines.

Many colleges and universities have at least one mainframe computer.

Minicomputers

These are usually about the size of a freezer chest and can serve the needs of tens of users at the same time via terminals. The difference between minis and mainframes is gradually becoming narrower as minis become more powerful. Many Psychology departments have their own minis.

Microcomputers and workstations

Microcomputers are complete computers (including VDU and disc drives) that normally fit on a desk top and are used by just one person at a time. They vary greatly in their speed and memory capacity. Very fast micros with high resolution graphics and large amounts of memory are often designated as **workstations**.

There are often several micros or workstations linked to a central computer (maybe a mainframe, a mini or another micro) that has a large disc drive to which they all have access. This central computer is known as a **file server**. The whole set-up is known as a **local area network** (**LAN**).

The distinction between the different kinds of computer is becoming increasingly blurred with ever more powerful micros offering the possibility of serving several users, super-minis being manufactured that are more like mainframes in terms of their power, desktop minis becoming available for single users, and so on. The remainder of this chapter focuses on mainframes (or super-minis), and a particular class of microcomputer.

1.5 Using mainframe computers

The statistics packages to be described in this book will run on most mainframes. The most commonly used mainframe in academic settings is the **VAX** made by the Digital Equipment Corporation. Also very popular are **IBM mainframes** or **Amdahls** ("copies" of IBM mainframes produced by a company whose founder was one of the main architects of the IBM series of mainframe computers).

Registering

To be able to use a mainframe computer you must first **register** as a user. This involves filling in a form and being assigned a **user number, user name, user id** or **job number** and a certain amount of space for your files on the computer's discs.

Once you have become a user, you are required to set a password that will have to be used at the start of each session. The reason for the password is not just to stop unwanted intrusions into your files. It is also to prevent hackers logging on to the mainframe in your name and using your account as a gateway to other user spaces and installations. **It is very important not to give your password to anyone else.** In doing so you will usually be violating an agreement that you signed when becoming a user of the computer installation.

Logging on and off

Every time you wish to begin a session at a terminal to a mainframe, you must go through a process know as **logging on**. This involves letting the computer know that you wish to use it and telling it your user name. It will then ask for your password and only if you type it in correctly will the computer accept you as a user. Once you have passed this hurdle you can type commands to the computer. When you have finished the session you **log off** or **log out**. This involves typing a command that tells the computer that you have finished with it for the time being.

1.6 Using microcomputers

PCs only

This book focuses exclusively on a class of microcomputers based on a configuration originally devised by IBM and copied by literally hundreds of manufacturers. This book will refer to IBM personal computers and their various copies as **IBM clones,** or **PCs** (personal computers). The statistics packages to be described will not work on other micros such as Apple Macintoshes.

At the risk of offending Macintosh owners there are no statistical packages yet available for these machines that match up to those available for the IBM clones.

Types of PC
PCs come in a number of guises. The basic format, however, is:

• a VDU;

• a box containing the main circuitry, including between 640 thousand bytes (**Kilobytes** or **KB**) and 16 MB of electronic memory (RAM), a small CPU on a single silicon chip and one or more disc drives;

• a printer connected to the main box by a cable.

The statistics packages to be described will run on all IBM clones. They will run quite slowly on those that use the slow **8088** CPU, slightly quicker on **8086**-based machines, much quicker on the **80286** machines (otherwise known as **AT** clones), and fastest of all on **80386** machines. At the time of writing, computers are beginning to come out with **80486** CPUs. These can be expected to work faster than all the others and still be fully compatible with them.

Types of disc drive
There are two main kinds of disc drive in use on IBM clones: **floppy disc** drives, and **hard disc** drives.

Floppy disc drives require you to insert floppy discs or **diskettes**. These are currently either **5.25"** or **3.5"** in diameter. They have relatively small capacity (between **360KB** and **1.4MB**) and are slow. The advantage is that you can have a library of floppy discs and just insert the one you wish to use. Also, you can carry your floppy discs around with you and use them on other PCs.

Hard discs are sealed into the disc drives and cannot be removed. They are fast and have a large capacity (normally between **20MB** and **120MB**). To use the statistics packages described in this book, you need to have a hard disc because the packages will not fit on a floppy. You will still need floppy discs, however, to keep copies of your data files in the event of the hard disc going wrong and losing all its files!

Buying a PC

If you are buying your own PC, the main decisions to make are:

* what kind of processor you want (8088, 80286, 80386 or 80486)

* what disc drives you want (3.5" and/or 5.25" floppies and 20, 40, 80 or 120MB hard disc)

* what kind of display you want (monochrome or colour, and if colour whether you want low resolution CGA, high resolution EGA or very high resolution VGA)

Currently the best value for money can probably be had with a 80386 PC with a 3.5" floppy drive and an 80MB hard drive with high resolution colour graphics. This configuration will do very nicely for running your statistical packages.

Before buying anything, you should get hold of computer magazines such as "Personal Computer World" or "Byte" and study the advertisements. If at all possible, take advice. Prices vary enormously for the same basic configuration.

Note: One important thing to bear in mind is that there is a high probability that your computer will not work when it arrives, or will break down in the first year. You can save yourself a great deal of trouble if you buy from a dealer who includes a 12 month on-site maintenance warranty in the price.

1.7 Operating systems

To make computers do things, you type commands on the keyboard. This may or may not result in something being displayed on the VDU.

Different computers have different sets of commands - even though the tasks that these commands perform may be the same.

Computers have to have a program running all the time that they are switched on to interpret your commands and execute them. This program is called the **operating system**. Most operating system commands relate to files on disc. They allow you to **copy** these files from one disc to another, **delete** files, obtain a **directory** of files, i.e. a list of what files there are on a disc, **display** the contents of text or data (ASCII) files on the VDU, **print** the contents of text or data (ASCII) files on paper, and **rename** files.

Stats packages and editors

Operating systems also allow you to enter a command that **runs a statistical package**. They also normally have a command that **runs an editor**. Editors are extremely important because they are the means by which you create and amend data files.

Remembering where you are

When you have typed a command to run a statistical package or editor, you are said to be **in** the package or editor. You then type further commands or text that gets the package or editor to do various useful things. When you have finished you type a command that allows you to **exit** back to the operating system. You are now **out of** the package or editor.

When you are using a computer, you need to remember **where you are in the system**. Are you in the operating system, in an editor or in a statistical package?

Prompts

The computer helps you remember where you are by displaying a **prompt** when it is waiting for you to type a command.

The operating system has a prompt called the **system prompt**. What this is depends on the computer. In the VAX's VMS operating system, the system prompt is the dollar sign ($). It tells you that you are in the operating system and not in an editor or a statistics package. The SPSS prompt on mainframes is *SPSS-X>*. This tells you that you are in SPSS and therefore can only use commands that SPSS understands, not operating system commands.

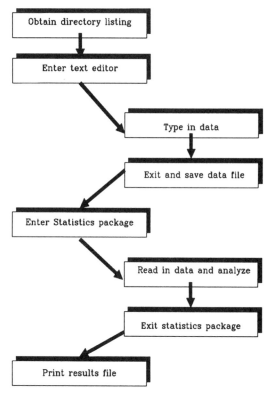

Figure 1.3 Schematic representation of a typical session. The user first of all has a look at what files there are on the disc then enters the text editor to create a new file containing some data. He/she then has to leave the text editor before he/she can go into the statistics package and carry out analysis on the data file. He/she then leaves the statistics package and prints out a file that has been created containing the results of the analysis.

A typical session

Figure 1.3 shows schematically a typical session in which a user types in an operating system command to list the names of the files on a disc, then goes into an editor, then leaves the editor returning him/her to the operating system. From there he goes into a statistical package. He/she then leaves SPSS bringing him back to the operating system. This allows him/her then to use an operating system command to print out a file containing the results of the statistical analysis (this file was created by the statistical package).

Kinds of operating system

Two of the most commonly used operating systems in use in Psychology departments at present are probably **MSDOS** for IBM clones, and **VMS** for VAX mainframes. In fact the commands for the two are quite similar - but there are differences and Appendices 1 and 2 provide an introduction to these two operating systems. If your mainframe is not a VAX then you will need to take advice from the advisory centre in your institution as to what computer and operating system you have. You will need to do this after reading this chapter and before going on to the rest of the book.

1.8 Conventions used in this book

When giving examples in a book on computing, it is necessary to show what the computer is displaying on the screen, and what you are supposed to type in. I have chosen to use *italics* on the left of the page to indicate the prompt that the computer will display, and ordinary text to show what you should type in.

When it comes to typing commands or file names into the computer it does not matter whether you use lower case or capitals; the computer treats them just the same. I use capitals for the sake of consistency.

Note: SPSS and MINITAB allow you to abbreviate commands. For example, the full command to obtain a Kruskal-Wallace analysis in MINITAB is KRUSKAL-WALLACE, but this can be shortened to KRUS. I have generally taken advantage of this facility in the examples in this book.

1.9 When typing commands into the computer...

Commands should be typed in exactly as shown, leaving spaces where spaces are shown in the example, and pressing the **Enter** key (sometimes labelled as **Return** or with an arrow) to end each line (see Figure 1.2).

Until you have pressed the Enter key the computer will allow you to go back **on that line** using the Backspace key (**BkSp**) and retype the command. Sometimes the Backspace key is marked by a left pointing arrow. Once the Enter key has been pressed the command will be executed or an error message will be displayed to indicate that there was something wrong with it.

You should note that the Backspace key is different from the **left cursor** key (see Figure 1.2). The latter is located with the other cursor keys. The Backspace key is normally located at the top right of the keyboard. If you use the left cursor key instead of the Backspace key, you may find that it does not rub out the characters as you would wish, but merely moves the cursor back over them.

When you press keys on the computer keyboard, if the key is Control, Shift, Caps or Alt, you hold it down while you press the key what goes with it (see Appendix 1 and 2). When you press any of the other keys, you must make sure that you press the key sharply, just once and **do not keep your finger on it**. This is because your computer keyboard will almost certainly have an **auto-repeat** facility in which if you leave the key pressed for more than half a second, the character is assumed to be repeatedly typed until you release the key. This can have undesirable effects.

1.10 Overview of SPSS

SPSS stands for Statistical Package for the Social Sciences. It comes in a mainframe version called **SPSS-X** and a microcomputer version called **SPSSPC+**.

The commands for the two versions are nearly identical. This makes my task that much easier. In this book, the commands for SPSS-X will be given. Only where the commands for SPSSPC+ differ will these be provided as well.

What can SPSS do?

SPSS-X can be used to carry out a wide range of statistical operations. It can calculate descriptive statistics including means, standard deviations, percentages, standard errors of the mean, and Pearson and Spearman correlations. It can also perform most of the statistical tests that psychologists use including t-tests (independent and related), analysis of variance (ANOVA) with multi-way factorial designs, unequal cell sizes and repeated measures, and non-parametric tests such as Chi-square tests for two-way contingency tables and log-linear analysis of multi-way contingency tables, Mann-Whitney, Wilcoxon, Kruskal-Wallace and Friedman.

With the analysis of variance, it is possible to specify a set of planned comparisons (although these are somewhat cumbersome) and post hoc multiple comparisons such as Scheffe's procedure. SPSS-X can also be used to carry out multivariate analyses including: principal components and factor analysis with various options for extraction and rotation methods; multiple regression analysis; cluster analysis and discriminant function analysis.

SPSSPC+ has all these facilities although for some of them it is necessary to purchase extra modules.

1.11 An overview of MINITAB

MINITAB was originally developed at Pennsylvania State University as an aid to teaching statistics. Its statistical functions are much more limited than those of SPSS but it is also easier to use. There are a large number of statistics courses in Psychology that use MINITAB.

Minitab was first developed for PDP-11 minicomputers. It has now been made available for a wide range of mainframes and, like SPSS, it has been converted to run on PCs. The PC version is slightly more limited than the mainframe version, but the commands are nearly the same.

Given that most readers of this book will be using the mainframe version of MINITAB, I will concentrate on this, but where commands for the microcomputer version differ, these will be given as well.

What MINITAB can do

MINITAB can be used for simple descriptive statistics such as frequencies, means, and standard deviations. Pearson correlations can be calculated and, with a bit of additional work, so can Spearman rank order correlations. MINITAB can carry out simple independent t-tests and, again with some extra work, related t-tests. There are facilities for one-way and multi-way ANOVAs. In the case of multi-way ANOVAs there must be the same number of subjects in each group. Non-parametric tests include the Chi-square test for two-way contingency tables, Wilcoxon, Kruskal-Wallace and Friedman. Multiple regression is very easy using MINITAB.

1.12 Updates of SPSS and MINITAB

Statistical packages, like any other software product, are continually being updated. This potentially poses problems for books such as this. However, the changes are usually enhancements involving the addition of extra commands so the commands given here should still work unless there is a major change in the way commands have to be given.

The versions used in the book are the most recent ones as at September 1990.

1.13 The Master Plan

This is how you analyze data using SPSS or MINITAB. Everything in this book is directed to helping you carry out these operations.

Note: You should keep referring back to this plan when you are in any doubt about what you are supposed to be doing.

The Master Plan consists of a set of operations. The order in which these are carried out and whether a particular operation is carried out will depend on your requirements.

A.   BEGIN A SESSION

Sit at a terminal or PC

Make sure it is switched on

If you are on a terminal, log on (Appendix 1)

B.   CREATE A DATA FILE

Go into a text editor (Appendix 1 or 2)

Type in data (Chapter 2 and Appendix 1 or 2)

Leave the text editor (Appendix 1 or 2)

C.   ANALYZE DATA IN A DATA FILE (Requires B. completed)

Go into SPSS or MINITAB (Appendix 1 or 2)

Read data from the data file into the workspace (Chapter 2)

*Possibly carry out transformations on the data in the workspace (Chapter 3)

*Possibly save a system file (Chapter 4)

Carry out analyses (e.g. means, t-tests, correlations etc.) (Chapters 5 to 13)

Exit from SPSS or MINITAB (Appendix 1 or 2)

D.   *POSSIBLY AMEND DATA FILE (Requires B. completed)

Go into text editor (Appendix 1 or 2)

Amend file (Appendix 1 or 2)

Leave text editor (Appendix 1 or 2)

E.   *POSSIBLY EXAMINE RESULTS FILE (Requires C. completed)

Go into text editor (Appendix 1 or 2)

View file (Appendix 1 or 2)

Leave text editor (Appendix 1 or 2)

*Possibly print results file (Appendix 1 or 2)

F.   ENDING A SESSION

If you are at a terminal, log off (Appendix 1)

Asterisks represent operations that you do not need to perform.

Note: You can begin and end a session at any time. You need not create your data file and analyze it all in the same session.

1.14 Before continuing

If you are using SPSS-X on a VAX mainframe whose operating system is VMS, you should turn to Appendix 1 before going on to Chapter 2.

If you are using MINITAB on a VAX mainframe whose operating system is VMS, you should turn to Appendix 1 before going on to Chapter 2.

If you are using SPSSPC+ on a PC whose operating system is MSDOS you should turn to Appendix 2 before going on to Chapter 2.

If you are using MINITAB on a PC whose operating system is MSDOS you should turn to Appendix 2 before going on to Chapter 2.

If you are using either SPSS-X or MINITAB on a mainframe other than a VAX whose operating system is VMS, you should consult your computer advisory service or course organiser who will give you the necessary instructions to create and amend data files, begin and end an SPSS-X session, and print results files. Everything else will be as specified in this book.

If you want to get right into trying things out you could turn to Appendix 3 to see examples of complete sessions.

Chapter 2

Creating and reading
in data files

This chapter tells you how to take data from your studies and make up a computer file containing those data so that they can be used for statistical analysis. It will then explain how to **read in** data from your data file. Reading in involves taking the data in the form of ASCII characters (see Chapter 1) and putting it into a **workspace** in a form which the package concerned (SPSS or MINITAB) can use.

Before you create a data file, you need to get your data in a form which is suitable for analysis.

2.1 Preparing data for entry into the computer

Step 1 is to convert all non-numeric data into numbers. For example, the sex of each subject could be coded as 1 for males and 2 for females (it is up to you what code you use so long as you remember which is which).

Step 2 is to determine the **variables** which you have collected for each **person** in your study (otherwise referred to as a **case** or **subject**). For example, suppose you have given out a questionnaire with 20 items and you also have information on the age and sex of your subjects, you would have a total of 22 variables. You should also have a unique **subject number** identifying each subject. With the subject number, age, sex and the 20 responses per questionnaire, each subject is providing 23 variables.

Step 3 is to see whether you have any **missing values**. These are variables for which data were not collected for one or more subjects. For example, when you send out postal questionnaires, respondents sometimes fail to respond to some items. There are therefore data missing for these variables. If you have missing values you should use a number which you are not using for anything else - you cannot just leave these numbers out. If, for example, the responses on the 20 item questionnaire mentioned above should be ratings from 1 to 5 (a Likert scale for example) and some subjects fail to answer some questions, you can enter a 9 for the missing data.

As you will see later, when you use the data in a statistical package you can tell the package to treat this number as a **missing value code**.

2.2 Entering data into the computer

Now you are ready to **enter** the data into the computer. This means using a **text editor** to create an ASCII file to hold your data. This file will be held on computer disc. The data will typed be subject by subject, with the variables **in the same order** for every subject.

As an example, data may be typed into a data file exactly as shown below:

```
001 34 1 .23 .34
002 36 2 .20 .18
003 37 1 .30 .41
004 23 2 .22 .99
005 40 1 .25 .34
```

In this example there are data from five subjects. The first variable is subject number, the second is age and the third is sex (coded as 1 for males and 2 for females). The remaining two variables are simple reaction times in seconds taken in the morning and the afternoon. Notice that there is a .99 in the data - this is a missing value where the subject concerned failed to turn up for the afternoon session. It is not to be taken literally but treated as a missing value code.

There must be exactly the same number of variables for every single subject. If you have more variables for some subjects than others, you must use missing value codes in places where there are real data from the other subjects.

The order in which the variables appear must be exactly the same for each subject.

You can use more than one line per case
Sometimes there are so many variables that the data for each subject cannot all be fitted on to one line. **This does not matter**. You can use as many lines as you like for each subject. As you will see later, the computer can be told how many variables to look for and where to find them.

EXAMPLE.DAT
The remaining examples in this book will use a data file called EXAMPLE.DAT which contains fictitious data from a study on the effect of various manipulations on cigarette craving in different kinds of smoker.

This data file is given in full in Appendix 4. You should now turn to Appendix 4 and with the assistance of Appendix 1 or 2 (depending on whether you are using a VAX or PC) you can create this file. If you are using a PC, I will assume that you have stored the file on a floppy disc which you will insert in drive A:.

2.3 Reading data into SPSS

The easiest way to read data into SPSS is by using **freefield format**. Later in this chapter I will tell you how to use **fixed format** read-in. This can be useful in some circumstances.

The first thing to do is obviously to get into SPSS. You should already know how to do this (see Appendix 1 for SPSS-X or Appendix 2 for SPSSPC+).

I will assume from now onwards that you are in SPSS. Thus you will be looking at the *SPSS-X>* prompt if you are working with SPSS-X, or the *SPSS/PC:* prompt if you are using SPSSPC+.

Note: If you are using the Review editor in SPSSPC+, you will not see any prompt when you are typing commands in.

Reading in EXAMPLE.DAT
Suppose that you want to do some analysis on the data in EXAMPLE.DAT. You would use the **DATA LIST** command as follows:

```
SPSS-X> DATA LIST FILE=EXAMPLE.DAT FREE / SUBNO CRAV1 DIFF1
CONT>    CRAV2 DIFF2 CRAV3 DIFF3 CRAV4 DIFF4 SEX COND AGE CO
CONT>    PSY HAND INDUL SED STIM AUTO ADD DEPEND CIGSPD
CONT>    MOTIV TROUB.
```

Note: You may need to type something different from **FILE=EXAMPLE.DAT** if you are not using a VAX mainframe. You will need to consult your course organiser or computer centre for the correct way to deal with files.

In the case of SPSSPC+, the command is the same except that you will have to tell the computer that the file is on a disc in the A: drive.

```
SPSS/PC:DATA LIST FILE='A:EXAMPLE.DAT' FREE / SUBNO
CONT>    CRAV1 DIFF1 CRAV2 DIFF2 CRAV3 DIFF3 CRAV4 DIFF4
CONT>    SEX COND AGE CO PSY HAND INDUL SED STIM
CONT>    AUTO ADD DEPEND CIGSPD MOTIV TROUB.
```

Note: It does not matter where you end each line. If you can type the whole lot on one line, then fine. Otherwise just use the Enter key to end each line at a convenient point (between words). SPSS will not try to execute the command until you have typed in a full stop. When you press the Enter key it will prompt you with CONT> or CONTINUE>.

The single quotes around the file name are needed in SPSSPC+. The key to press is the one on the lower right of the keyboard. There may be another single quote key at the top right or top left of the keyboard, but this must not be used.

The only parts of this command that you need to change for your own real-life data files are: the name of the file containing the data (EXAMPLE.DAT), and the variable names (SUBNO, CRAV1 etc.).

Variable names

You can make the variable names whatever you like as long as they have no more than eight characters and begin with a letter. I have chosen names which make it reasonably clear what the variables are but you could have something like:

SPSS-x> DATA LIST FILE=EXAMPLE.DAT FREE / V1 TO V24.

This will read in 24 variables with the names V1, V2, V3 etc. As you will see, it saves typing but the penalty is that you need to keep a record on a piece of paper of what V1, V2 etc. refer to.

The word **TO** can be used as a shorthand when you have a variable name ending with a number (as in V1 TO V24). It is just a way of saving typing.

Do not forget that SPSS will not know that you have finished typing in a command until you put in a full stop followed by Enter.

Error checking

Your data may not be read in properly the first time. You may, for example, have made an error when typing the numbers into the data file, or you may have made a mistake when typing the DATA LIST command.

If SPSS detects something seriously wrong with the data file when reading it in, it may give an **error** message, or a **warning**. If you get an error message or a warning, you **must** check it out. You should examine the data file to make sure that there are no non-numeric characters in it, that all the numbers are in their correct places, and that you have not accidentally left out a number or typed in too many numbers.

Non-numeric characters can appear because you have typed a capital O instead of a zero, or a lower case L instead of a 1.

One way of checking your data is to LIST the subject numbers - that is one reason for having them in the data file in the first place. Once you have used the DATA LIST command to read the data in, you should always type the command:

SPSS-X> LIST VAR=SUBNO.

Note: This assumes that you have used the name SUBNO in the DATA LIST command to denote the variable containing subject numbers. You can use whatever name you like (e.g. V1).

If in the resulting output, the subject numbers do not appear in the order in which they occur in the data file, then you know that something has gone wrong. Moreover, you can tell where the problem lies by looking for the point where the list deviates from what it should be.

Once you have executed this command, your data will be in the SPSS workspace, ready for the next stage in the operation.

2.4 Reading data into MINITAB

You should know by now how to get into MINITAB (see Appendix 1 for the mainframe version or Appendix 2 for the PC version). I will assume from now on that you are in MINITAB and are looking at the MINITAB prompt *MTB>*.

To read in data you use the **READ** command. This is easiest to explain by means of an example. You should have created the data file called EXAMPLE.DAT described earlier. We will use this example.

Reading in EXAMPLE.DAT

The command to read this data into MINITAB could be:

MTB>   READ 'EXAMPLE.DAT' C1-C24

This is the same for PC and VAX mainframes, except that the PC version requires you to indicate that the file is on a disc in drive A:.

MTB>   READ 'A:EXAMPLE.DAT' C1-C24

Note: The single quotes around the file name are the ones located on the bottom left of the keyboard (see Chapter 1).

If you are using a mainframe other than a VAX, you may need to substitute something else for **'EXAMPLE.DAT'**.

The only parts of this command that you need to change for your own real life data are the name of the file containing the data (EXAMPLE.DAT) and the number of variables you wish to read in. In MINITAB, all variables are denoted by C followed by a number. Thus the first variable (subject number in this case), is C1, the second is C2 and so on.

This is different from SPSS where you can specify your own variable names. In MINITAB it is possible using a further set of commands to give your variables more readable names, but it is rarely worth it. It is best just to keep a separate note of what C1, C2 etc. refer to.

The hyphen (-) between C1 and C24 indicates that the computer is to give the names C2, C3, C4, C5, C6, C7, C8 etc. to variables in between. Note that this is different from SPSS which uses the word **TO** for this purpose.

Unlike SPSS, MINITAB commands do not use full stops to tell the computer that the end of the command has been reached. MINITAB assumes that the end of the command is signalled by pressing the Enter key.

This means that commands normally have to be contained on one line. Because MINITAB commands are so concise, this is usually not a problem. However, if you do need to go over to the next line, you tell the computer that you are doing this by having an ampersand symbol (&) as the last character on the line. Thus you could have:

```
MTB>    READ 'EXAMPLE.DAT' C1 C2 C3 C4 C6 C7 C8 C9 &
CONT>   C10 C11 C12 C13 C14 C15-C24.
```

Even with the ampersand, you are limited to lines of no more than 80 characters. In addition you may not be able to read more than 100 variables in at a time (depending on what computer you are working on).

A serious limitation concerns the number of lines per subject in the **data file**. Using this form of READ command you can only read in one line of data per subject. Thus if you have a large number of variables per subject and these will not all fit on one line, you will have, either to break the data file up or to use a more advanced form of READ command described below.

Error checking

Your data may not be read in properly the first time. You may, for example, have made an error when typing the numbers into the data file, or you may have made a mistake when typing the READ command.

If MINITAB detects something seriously wrong with the data file when reading it in, it may give an **error** message, or a **warning**. If you get an error message or a warning, you **must** check it out. You should examine the data file to make sure that there are no non-numeric characters in it, that all the numbers are in their correct places, and that you have not accidentally left out a number or typed in too many numbers.

Non-numeric characters can appear because you have typed a capital O instead of a zero, or a lower case L instead of a 1.

One way of checking your data is to LIST the subject numbers - that is one reason for having them in the data file in the first place. Once you have used the READ command to read the data in, you should always type the command:

MTB>   PRINT C1.

This assumes that you have used C1 to hold your subject numbers.

If in the resulting output the subject numbers do not appear in the order in which they occur in the data file, then you know that something has gone wrong. Moreover, you can tell where the problem lies by looking for the point where the list deviates from what it should be.

You know enough about reading data into MINITAB to be able to go on to the next chapter. The following sections are for more advanced read-in operations.

2.5 More advanced use of commands to read in data

The commands described above will do fine for almost all purposes. You should make sure that you understand how they work and only read this section if the need arises or if you are fully conversant with the simpler forms of command.

SPSS - formatted data read-in

There are two main circumstances when the method of reading data in described above will not be of any use:

1.   when you do not have spaces between your variables in the data file

2.   when you want to skip over some variables.

In these cases you need to use a **formatted** read command. This is otherwise know as a **fixed format** read command.

In formatted read, you have to tell SPSS where to look for each of the variables you want to read in.

Going back to the data file, EXAMPLE.DAT. The equivalent formatted read command would be:

```
SPSS-X> DATA LIST FILE=EXAMPLE.DAT FIXED/ SUBNO 1-2
CONT>   CRAV1 4 DIFF1 6 CRAV2 8 DIFF2 10 CRAV3 12 DIFF3 14
CONT>   CRAV4 16 DIFF4 18 SEX 20 COND 22 AGE 24-25 CO
CONT>   27-28 PSY 29 HAND 31 INDUL 33 SED 35 STIM 37 AUTO
CONT>   39 ADD 41 DEPEND 43-44 CIGSPD 46-47 MOTIV
CONT>   49 TROUB 51.
```

Each variable name is followed by a specification of the column or columns in which it is located on the data file, with the far left margin being column 1 and the far right usually being column 80. Notice that the statement is much longer and more cumbersome than the freefield read command.

It is sometimes possible to make formatted read commands somewhat shorter by lumping a whole lot of consecutive variables together.

Thus you may notice that CRAV1, DIFF1 etc. to DIFF4 are all one digit in length with a single space between them. Here is a shortened form of the read command which takes advantage of this:

```
SPSS-X> DATA LIST FILE=EXAMPLE.DAT FIXED / SUBNO 1-2
CONT>   CRAV1 DIFF1 CRAV2 DIFF2 CRAV3 DIFF3 CRAV4 DIFF4
CONT>   3-18 SEX 20 COND 22 AGE 24-25 CO 27-28 PSY 29 HAND
CONT>   31 INDUL 33 SED 35 STIM 37 AUTO 39 ADD 41 DEPEND
CONT>   43-44 CIGSPD 46-47 MOTIV 49 TROUB 51.
```

Consider the list going from CRAV1 to DIFF4. The way this works is to treat each of the numbers as though they were two-digit numbers right next to each other (i.e. with no spaces between them) starting on column 3. Of course the first digit of the two digit numbers will always be blank but that does not matter. Then instead of giving the individual column numbers for each variable in the list you just have to specify the start column number of the first variable (column 3) and the end column number of the last variable (column 18).

Note: Remember that this system is only there for your convenience. If you do not understand how it works, you do not need to use it.

Because the column numbers are specified in the read statement, you do not need to have spaces between the variables. Thus you could have a data file called NEWDAT.DAT whose contents looked like this:

```
01132454
02234231
03243233
04233242
```

which consisted of six variables: subject number (2 digits), condition (1 digit), three sets of ratings (each of 1 digit), and age (2 digits). This could be read in by the command:

```
SPSS-X> DATA LIST FILE=NEWDAT.DAT FIXED / SUBNO 1-2
CONT>   COND 3 RATING1 TO RATING3 4-6 AGE 7-8.
```

Reading in **floating point** numbers (i.e. numbers with decimal points in them), need be no different from reading in integers (those without decimal points). For example, suppose we had a file called NEWDAT2.DAT laid out as follows:

```
001 23.4 12.45
002  3.2 99.54
003 12.3 78.23
```

This could be read in using the command:

```
SPSS-X> DATA LIST FILE = NEWDAT2.DAT FIXED/SUBNO 1-3 V1
CONT>   5-8 V2 10-14.
```

When data for each subject go on to more than one line you simply tell SPSS to move on to the next line by using the slash character (/).

Thus suppose you have a file called NEWDAT3.DAT laid out as follows:

```
01 23 2 2 2 2 3 2 3 2 4 34 56 5 3
   23 45 34 34 456 56 3 33
02 21 3 3 3 3 3 3 3 2 3 44 54 3 2
   55 32 36 23 423 23 3 56
```

This could be read in by the command:

```
SPSS-X> DATA LIST FILE=NEWDAT3.DAT FIXED/ SUBNO 1-2
CONT>   AGE 4-5 V1 TO V9 6-23 V10 25-26 V11 28-29 V12 31 V13
CONT>   23 / V14 TO V17 3-14 V18 16-18 V19 20-21
CONT>   V20 23 V21 25-26.
```

The slash occurs between V13 and V14 to indicate that a new line has been started.

The variables V14 to V17 are read in together as though they were all three-digit numbers starting on column 3 and ending on column 14, with the first digit of each variable being blank. This is another example of the shorthand technique described earlier.

The slash is needed in the fixed format read command but note that it is <u>not</u> needed in the freefield read described in the main part of this chapter.

Although the fixed format read command does give greater

flexibility than the freefield read, as long as you organise your data file appropriately when you start out, you should never need to use it. So do not worry if you have found these last few paragraphs difficult to follow.

MINITAB - formatted read-in

MINITAB uses a somewhat different form of formatted read command from that used in SPSS. It is based on the read command used in a computer programming language called FORTRAN. (This is the language in which MINITAB is written.)

Going back to EXAMPLE.DAT, the MINITAB formatted read command would be:

```
MTB>   READ 'EXAMPLE.DAT' C1-C24;
SUBC>  FORMAT (F2.0,10(X,F1.0),2(X,F2.0),&
CONT>  7(X,F1.0),2(X,F2.0),2(X,F1.0)).
```

Put A: before EXAMPLE.DAT if you are using the PC. This all looks very complicated but it is not as bad as it seems.

First of all, notice that you put a semicolon at the end of the line containing READ. This tells MINITAB that you want to use one of the subcommands that is available. It brings up the *SUBC>* prompt.

You then type FORMAT which tells MINITAB that you want describe the format in which the data appear in the data file.

What comes next works as foilows:

The formula is to be read from left to right and goes through the variables for each subject from left to right, starting at the left hand margin of the data file.

X means skip a space.

F1.0 means read a variable which is one digit long and has no digits after a decimal place.

F2.0 means read a variable which is two digits long and has no digits after the decimal place.

Commas are always used to separate Xs and Fs.

A number in front of an X, F or set of brackets means repeat whatever follows a particular number of times. Thus 2X means skip two spaces. Also 10(X,F1.0) means repeat "skip a space and then read a one digit variable" ten times. Thus it reads ten variables each separated by a space.

Whenever an F is encountered it is assumed to refer to the next variable in the list of variables given in the READ command (e.g. C1-C24). Thus the first F2.0 will read the variable in that position into C1, the next ten Fs will read the single digit numbers from the data file into C2 to C11, and so on.

Note: I said before that MINITAB commands do not generally end in a full stop. The exception is when you use a subcommand, as in the FORMAT statement. To let MINITAB know that you have finished with all possible subcommands, you must use a full stop.

I had to use the & sign at the end of the first line of the FORMAT statement because it would not all fit on one line. It is important to note, that the FORMAT statement can be no more than 80 characters in all, even if it goes on to another line. This is an irritating limitation of MINITAB.

You will probably be able to see how the formatted read command in MINITAB gives the same kind of flexibility as its equivalent in SPSS. You can have your variables right next to each other without spaces in between. You can also skip over spaces and numbers if you want to.

Take the data file NEWDAT.DAT used previously. There are

no spaces between the variables. The MINITAB command to read this in would be:

```
MTB>    READ 'NEWDAT.DAT' C1-C6;
SUBC>   FORMAT (F2.0,4F1.0,F2.0).
```

To read in floating point numbers, you simply have to remember to indicate how many digits come after the decimal point. Thus, to read in the data file NEWDAT2.DAT described above you would use:

```
MTB>    READ 'NEWDAT2.DAT' C1-C3;
SUBC>   FORMAT (F3.0,X,F4.1,X,F5.2).
```

Data on more than one line

Because of all the complexities, I try to avoid using formatted read commands in MINITAB but there is one situation I encounter when it cannot be avoided - that is when each subject has so much data that they cannot all be fitted on to one line. In SPSS you could still use freefield read commands but unfortunately in MINITAB you cannot. The way that a new line is signalled in MINITAB format statements is, as with SPSS, by means of a slash. Thus to read in the file NEWDAT3.DAT given previously, you would type:

```
MTB>    READ 'NEWDAT3.DAT' C1-C21;
SUBC>   FORMAT (2(F2.0,X),9(F1.0,X),&
CONT>   2(F2.0,X),2(F1.0,X),/,&
CONT>   3X,4(F2.0,X),F3.0,F2.0).
MTB>    READ 'NEWDAT3.DAT' C22 C23;
SUBC>   FORMAT (/,22X,F1.0,X,F2.0).
```

I had to use two read commands to get the data in because the FORMAT statement to read the whole lot in one go would exceed the 80 character limit.

In the first read command we stop at variable C21. In the second read command we begin with variable C22. But we have to tell the computer where to begin read that variable; therefore we have a slash at the beginning of the FORMAT statement to tell it to move to the second line and then we tell it to skip 22 spaces before starting to reading the variable C22.

Formatted read commands in MINITAB take some getting used to so you may wish to avoid them wherever possible. If you have a data set in which one line per subject would not be enough, you can always make up two or more data files, each with just one line per subject, and then read in these files one after the other with, for example, C1-C20 coming from data file 1, C21-C40 from data file 2 and so on.

Note: As long as you use different variable names (C numbers) for each different READ command, successive READ commands will not wipe out the previous ones. This is very different from SPSS where every DATA LIST command automatically wipes out the workspace created by a previous DATA LIST command.

2.6 Conclusion

This chapter has instructed you on how to read data from a data file into the workspace of SPSS or MINITAB. If you keep to freefield format, this can be a simple command of one or two lines. If you have to use fixed format, things get a bit more complicated.

Once data have been read into the workspace, they may be able to be analyzed straight away using the commands given in Chapters 5 to 13. However, there will be many occasions when you have to perform some transformations on the data first. This is covered in the next chapter.

Chapter 3

Recoding, transforming and selecting data

Once you have read data into the workspace in an SPSS or MINITAB session (see previous Chapter), you **may** need to carry out some transformations on it before it can be used. On the other hand you may not. This chapter only applies if you have data that need some kind of transformation before use.

Handling missing data and recoding variables

You read in the previous chapter that when there are missing data it is necessary to give these a numeric value called the **missing value code** and then to tell the statistical package to treat this as missing data.

This is just one kind of **recode** operation which you can get the computer to perform. Recode operations change values of variables according to some rule which you specify. For example, you may have a variable containing the number of cigarettes the subjects smoke per day, and want instead to have a variable which just indicates whether or not they are smokers.

Transforming variables

There may also be occasions when you want to apply some mathematical operation on the data in some way before analyzing it. Perhaps the most common example, is the need to take the square roots or logs of reaction time data to "normalize" the distribution and make the data suitable for parametric statistical tests (e.g. t-tests and ANOVAs, see later chapters).

Combining variables

You may also want to combine variables in an arithmetic expression. For example, one often wishes to add sets of ratings together to derive a total score for a questionnaire (as with a Likert scale), or a set of subscale scores (as with the General Health Questionnaire and Eysenck Personality Questionnaire).

Selecting cases for analysis

Finally, there will be occasions when you want to perform an analysis separately on different groups of subjects. For example, one might wish to examine the relationship between age and number of road traffic accidents per year for drivers separately in different age ranges, 17 to 24, 24 to 60, and 60 upwards. Alternatively one might wish to examine it separately for males and females. This involves the selection of cases according to certain criteria. SPSS and MINITAB have special commands to enable you to select cases for analysis.

3.1 Recoding missing values in SPSS

In EXAMPLE.DAT there were some missing values which were indicated by using a 9 for single digit numbers (e.g. CRAV1) and 99 (e.g. AGE) for double digit numbers.

For the remainder of this chapter, I will assume that you have already created the file EXAMPLE.DAT, started up SPSS-X or SPSSPC+, and used the DATA LIST command given in Chapter 2 to read the data into the SPSS workspace. (Remember that you have to read the data in every time you begin a session with SPSS.)

Once you have read the data in using DATA LIST, you can tell SPSS to treat 9s and 99s as missing values as follows:

```
SPSS-X> MISSING VALUES CRAV1 TO DIFF4 SEX (9) AGE CO
CONT>   CIGSPD (99).
```

This tells SPSS to treat 9 as a missing value in the variables CRAV1 DIFF1 CRAV2 ... DIFF4 and for SEX. It also tells SPSS to treat 99 as a missing value for the variables AGE, CO and CIGSPD.

You can specify lots of different missing values for different variables using this command. You put the variables to be recoded first and then in brackets the missing value code which applies to those variables, then the next list of variables followed by their missing value codes and so on.

I did not include the variables PSY to ADD in the command because in these variables, 9 is a real score (the scale goes from 0 to 9). If we had had any missing values in these variables, it would have been necessary to use a two digit number as the missing value code which would have meant having an extra space to leave room for it if all the numbers were to line up (not strictly necessary with the freefield read command, but useful when visually inspecting the data file for errors).

3.2 Computing new scores in SPSS

Suppose that you wished to combine the ratings of craving and difficulty not smoking at each abstinence point into a single score by adding them. SPSS allows arithmetic operations to be performed on variables using the COMPUTE command. Thus we could have:

```
SPSS-X>  COMPUTE CRAVTOT1 = CRAV1 + DIFF1.
```

This would add up CRAV1 and DIFF1 for each subject and put the result into a new variable called CRAVTOT1.

You can choose any name you like for the new variable (up to eight characters long). Once it has been created, it can be used just like any other variable for the remainder of the session.

The COMPUTE command can use any of the usual arithmetic **operators** (addition, subtraction, multiplication and division). A hyphen (-) is used as a minus sign, an asterisk (*) for the multiplication sign, and a slash (/) for the division sign. You can also use brackets to make sure that operations are carried out in the right order. In the absence of brackets, multiplication and division are carried out before addition and subtraction.

Examples of arithmetic expressions

Here are some simple examples of arithmetic expressions just to show you how it works:

6+4/2   gives 8 because 4 is divided by 2 to give 2 and then 6 is added.

(6+4)/2   gives 5 because 6 is added to 4 to give 10 and this is then divided by 2.

6+4*2   gives 14 because 4 is multiplied by 2 to give 8 which is then added to 6.

(6+4)*2   gives 20 because 6 is added to 4 to give 10 which is then multiplied by 2.

Using arithmetic expressions

Suppose that you wished to calculate the mean (average) composite craving score for each subject across the four abstinence points, you could use:

SPSS-X> COMPUTE CRAVMEAN = (CRAV1+CRAV2+CRAV3+CRAV4)/4.

Spaces in such expressions are optional.

Suppose that you wished to calculate the change from CRAV1 to CRAV2, you could type in the command:

SPSS-X> COMPUTE CRAVCHAN = CRAV1 - CRAV2.

Apart from the arithmetic operators, SPSS provides a set of **functions**, which can be used in COMPUTE statements. The most useful ones are:

SQRT   which calculates square roots
ABS   which turns negative numbers into positive ones
LG10   which takes logs to base 10
LN   which takes natural logs
RND   which rounds to the nearest whole number
TRUNC   which truncates to the next lowest integer

Functions are applied to an expression in brackets immediately following them. Thus, to compute a variable which is the square root of the CO value in EXAMPLE.DAT one would type the command:

SPSS-X> COMPUTE SQCO = SQRT(CO).

You should not have a space between the function name and the opening bracket.

Functions can be used in arithmetic expressions of any complexity, as in:

SPSS-X> COMPUTE COPERCIG = SQRT(CO/CIGSPD).

This would calculate the expired air carbon monoxide concentration divided by the number of cigarettes per day and then take the square root of the result.

Note: If a subject has any missing values in one or more of the variables used in a compute command, then the resulting variable will be set to a missing value for that subject. This makes sense because obviously the COMPUTE command will be missing crucial information on which to make its calculation.

3.3 Conditional compute commands in SPSS

You may want to transform variables or create new ones differently for different groups of subjects. Suppose for example, that women were known to have lower expired air carbon monoxide concentrations for a given amount of smoke inhaled than men. We might want to adjust the CO variable to make them comparable (rather like the adjustment that needs to be made in calculating blood alcohol concentrations from dose of alcohol consumed). Thus we might use:

SPSS-X> IF (SEX=1) CO=CO*1.2.

The part in brackets determines which subjects are affected by the transformation; the part after that specifies what the transformation is. In this case it involves changing an existing variable, but you could create a new variable just by using a name which is different from one of the existing variable names.

Thus if you wanted to keep the old CO variable, you could type the command:

SPSS-X> IF (SEX=1) CO2=CO*1.2.

You may be wondering what the value of CO2 will now be for those subjects for whom SEX was **not** 1 (i.e. the males). The answer is that it will be set to "missing". You can then type the command:

SPSS-X> IF (SEX=2) CO2=CO.

This will now fill in all the remaining values of CO2 making them equal to the value for CO for those subjects.

The expression which determines whose data are to be transformed (e.g. IF SEX=1) can include the following characters:

=	which means "is equal to"
>	which means "is greater than"
>=	which means "is greater than or equal to"
<	which means "is less than"
<=	which means "is less than or equal to"
<>	which means "is not equal to"
AND	which means "and"
OR	which means "or"

Suppose that you wished to calculate an adjusted CO index differently for different age bands, you might use the commands:

```
SPSS-X> IF (AGE>50) CO3=CO*1.4.
SPSS-X> IF ((AGE>30) AND (AGE<=50)) CO3=CO*1.2.
SPSS-X> IF (AGE<=30) CO3=CO.
```

Notice the use of brackets to make it clear how the expression should be interpreted. The use of the AND in the second command should need no explanation.

3.4 Recoding variables in SPSS

SPSS allows you to change the values of your variables in almost any way imaginable. Suppose that the craving scores had been coded in the original data file so that 1 referred to a high level of craving and 6 to a low level. We could reverse this as follows:

```
SPSS-X> RECODE CRAV1 CRAV2 CRAV3 CRAV4 (1=6) (2=5) (3=4)
CONT>   (4=3) (5=2) (6=1).
```

The general idea is that you give the list of variables you wish to recode (CRAV1 etc.), and then in separate brackets the transformations you wish to make. (1=6) means turn all 1s to 6s.

You can have as many RECODE commands as you like.

Suppose that you wanted to recode the age variable into three categories: under 30, 30 to 40 and over 40 years. You could use the RECODE command as follows:

```
SPSS-X> RECODE AGE (LOWEST THRU 29.9=1) (30 THRU 40=2)
CONT>   (40.1 THRU HIGHEST=3).
```

We were able to use the keywords LOWEST, THRU and HIGHEST to save a great deal of typing. The meaning of the keywords is obvious; remember that they must be spelt exactly as shown.

Once a variable has been recoded, it stays that way for the remainder of the session or until you perform another recode operation on it.

3.5 Selecting cases in SPSS

Sometimes you want to carry out operations on only some of the subjects. If you want permanently to select a subset of the subjects for the remainder of this session, you use the SELECT IF command, as in:

```
spss-x> SELECT IF (SEX=1).
```

From that point onwards, all the male subjects will have been deleted from the workspace. The expression in brackets can use any of the relational operators you saw in the conditional compute command (i.e. =, >, >=, <, <=, <>, AND, and OR).

The SELECT IF command is rather drastic because the deleted subjects cannot be recovered except by reading in the data file again using the DATA LIST command. To perform the selection temporarily (i.e. just for the next command) in SPSS-X you use the TEMPORARY command, as in:

```
spss-x> TEMPORARY.
spss-x> SELECT IF (SEX=1).
```

In this case the SELECT IF will only apply to whatever command comes next. Once that command has been completed the workspace will be back to its original state.

In SPSSPC+, there is no TEMPORARY command. The equivalent to TEMPORARY and SELECT IF together is the single command, PROCESS IF, as in:

```
spss/pc:PROCESS IF (SEX=1).
```

3.6 Recoding missing values in MINITAB

In EXAMPLE.DAT there were some missing values which were indicated by using a 9 for single digit numbers (e.g. C2) and 99 (e.g. C12) for double digit numbers. To tell MINITAB to treat these as missing values and not literally, we use the CODE command as follows:

```
MTB>    CODE (9) '*' C2-C11 C2-C11
MTB>    CODE (99) '*' C12 C13 C22 C12 C13 C22
```

This means: "with variables C2 to C11 turn any 9s into asterisks (MINITAB's special character to designate missing values) and put the result back into the original variables C2-C11; and with C12 C13 and C22 turn any 99s into asterisks and put the results back into C12, C13 and C22.

The reason that the variables are specified twice (e.g. there are two lots of C2-C11) is that the first set indicates the variables which are to be recoded, and the second set indicates where the results are to be put. Thus we could have had:

```
MTB>    CODE (9) '*' C2-C11 C102-C111
```

which would leave C2 to C11 unchanged and put the results of the missing value recode into variables C102 to C111.

Note: If you are running MINITAB on a computer which will only allow up to 100 variables, use of C102-C111 may not work. You could use C25-C34.

I did not include the variables C14 to C20 in the command because in these variables 9 is a real score (the scale goes from 0 to 9). If there had been any missing values in these variables, it would have been necessary to use a two digit number (e.g. 99).

3.7 Computing new scores in MINITAB

Suppose that you wished to combine the ratings of craving and difficulty not smoking after 24 hours' abstinence into a single score by simply adding them. MINITAB allows arithmetic operations to be performed on variables using the LET command. Thus we could have:

MTB>   `LET C25=C2+C3`

This would add up the 24 hour craving score (C2) and the difficulty not smoking score (C3) for each subject and put the result into a new variable called C25.

Note: Unlike SPSS all variable names must be C followed by a number. I chose 25 as the first number not being used for anything else.

The LET command can use any of the usual arithmetic **operators** (addition, subtraction, multiplication and division). A hyphen (-) is used as a minus sign, an asterisk (*) for the multiplication sign, and a slash (/) for the division sign. You can also use brackets to make sure that operations are carried out in the right order. In the absence of brackets, multiplication and division are carried out before addition and subtraction.

See Section 3.2 for examples of arithmetic expressions using these operators.

Suppose that you wished to calculate the mean (average) composite craving score for each subject across the four abstinence points, you could use:

MTB>   `LET C26=(C2+C4+C6+C8)/4`

Suppose that instead you wished to calculate the change in craving score from 24 hours (C2) to 48 hours (C4), you could type in the command:

MTB>   `LET C27=C2-C4`

Apart from the arithmetic operators, MINITAB provides you

with a set of "functions", which can be used in LET statements. The most useful ones are:

SQRT   which calculates square roots
ABSOLUTE   which turns negative numbers into positive ones
LOGTEN   which takes log to base 10
LOGE   which takes natural logs
ROUND   which rounds to the nearest whole number

Functions are applied to an expression in brackets immediately following them. Thus, to compute a variable which is the square root of the CO score in EXAMPLE.DAT you would type the command:

MTB>   LET C13=SQRT(C13)

The old C13 variable will be overwritten (replaced) by its square root because we have used the same variable name.

Functions can be used in arithmetic expressions of any complexity, as in:

MTB>   LET C28=SQRT(C13/C22)

This would calculate the expired air carbon monoxide concentration (C13) divided by the number of cigarettes per day (C22) and then take the square root of the result. It puts the result in a new variable, C28.

Note: If a subject has any missing values in one or more of the variables used in a compute command, then the resulting variable will be set to a missing value for that subject. This makes sense because obviously the LET command will be missing crucial information on which to make its calculation.

MINITAB has some arithmetic commands not available in SPSS but which are very useful. Suppose that you wished to add up the smoking motivation scores C14 to C20 to get a total score. You could type in the command:

```
MTB>    LET C29=C14+C15+C16+C17+C18+C19+C20
```

but MINITAB has a much more concise command, RSUM which is used as follows:

```
MTB>    RSUM C14-C20 C29
```

This means take the sum of C14 through to C20 then put the result in C29.

Another useful command is RSD. This calculates the standard deviation of a set of scores from the same subject, as in:

```
MTB>    RSD C14-C20 C30
```

which calculates for each subject the standard deviation of their smoking motivation scores and puts the result in C30. This can be used, for example, to calculate an index of variability in scores for use in subsequent analysis.

3.8 Recoding variables in MINITAB

MINITAB allows you to recode variables in a manner similar to that used in SPSS. Suppose that the craving scores had been coded in the original data file so that 1 referred to a high level of craving and 6 to a low level. We could reverse this as follows:

```
MTB>    CODE (1) 6 (2) 5 (3) 4 (4) 3 (5) 2 (6) 1 &
CONT>   C2 C4 C6 C8 C2 C4 C6 C8
```

The general idea is that you give the original values in brackets followed in each case by what you want to convert them to. Then you specify the list of variables you want this to apply to and finally the list of variables where the recoded values are to end up. In this example, the recoded values are to be put back into the original variables.

You can have as many CODE commands as you like.

Suppose that you wanted to recode the age variable into three categories: under 30, 30 to 40 and over 40 years. You could use the CODE command as follows:

```
MTB>    CODE (0:29.9) 1 (30:40) 2 (40.1:999) 3 C12 C12
```

You can use a colon (:) to indicate that all the numbers between 0 and 29.9 inclusive should be recoded to 1; (30:40) means all values between 30 and 40; (40.1:999) means all values between 40.1 and 999.

Remember that the first C12 indicates the variable to be recoded; the second indicates that the results are to be put back in the same variable they came from. Once a variable has been recoded, it stays that way for the remainder of the session or until you perform another recode operation on it.

3.9 Selecting cases in MINITAB

Sometimes you want to carry out operations on only some of the subjects. What you do in MINITAB is to copy values from one or more variables to another set of variables, selecting or omitting cases where variables have certain values.

Suppose that you wanted to select the males only. You could type in the command:

```
MTB>    COPY C1-C24 C101-C124;
SUBC>   CHOOSE (C10=2).
```

This means "copy the variables C1 to C24 to a new set of variables, C101 to C124, but only include cases where the value of C10 is 2 (i.e. sex is male)". In this case, wherever the sex is female a missing value will be generated. The old values of C1 to C24 remain.

You could have typed the command as follows:

```
MTB>    COPY C1-C24 C1-C24;
SUBC>   CHOOSE (C10=2).
```

c

This would have copied the variables C1 to C24 back on to themselves thus overwriting the original versions (i.e. deleting all cases where C10 was not 2).

Note: The semicolon at the end of the first line of the command tells MINITAB to expect a subcommand. That is why it comes up with the prompt *SUBC>*. To tell MINITAB that there are no more subcommands coming you must end the subcommand with a full stop.

MINITAB allows you to use the COPY command to leave out cases as well as select them. This is sometimes more convenient, although in principle the CHOOSE command is all that is actually required. Thus if you wanted to omit cases who were less than 30 years old you could type:

```
MTB>    COPY C1-C24 C1-C24;
SUBC>   OMIT (C12<30).
```

The same set of relational operators (<, >, <= etc.) are available to be used as with SPSS's SELECT IF command (see Section 3.3).

3.9 Conclusion

You have now seen how to create a data file for analysis, begin a session with SPSS or MINITAB, read data from data files into an SPSS or MINITAB workspace, declare any missing value codes, perform any necessary data transformations and select desired cases for analysis. There is one more thing to learn before going on to data analysis proper - that is how to save your SPSS or MINITAB workspace with all the transformations etc. so that you don't have to do these every time you start a new SPSS or MINITAB session. This is dealt with in the next chapter.

Chapter 4

Saving and restoring system files

In the last two chapters you saw how to read data from an ASCII file into SPSS or MINITAB and then how to recode and transform variables, compute new variables and select cases for separate analysis. These operations only stay in force until you finish the current session of SPSS or MINITAB. The next time you want to do some analysis on this data you will have to type in the recode, compute and select commands all over again.

System files
There is an alternative, however. At any time in an SPSS or MINITAB session, you can type in a command which saves as a **system file** the current workspace including all the variables you originally read in from the file plus any you have computed. It will also save the results of any recode commands. You can think of it as a snapshot of the state of the workspace **at the time you give the save command**. When you wish to use your data on another occasion you do not have to read them from the original ASCII file, you type in a very brief command which restores the system file you created. This puts you back exactly where you were at the time you saved the system file.

4.1 Saving and restoring system files in SPSS

You should by now have created the file EXAMPLE.DAT described in Appendix 4. You should also have tried out some or all of the RECODE and COMPUTE commands in Chapter 3. I will now assume that you have started up a session of SPSS and used the DATA LIST command to read in EXAMPLE.DAT. You might also have used the MISSING command to recode the missing values and typed in some of the other COMPUTE or RECODE commands given in the last chapter. We will now start from this point.

Saving system files

You can save the current state of the workspace using the command SAVE, as in:

spss-x> SAVE OUTFILE=EXAMPLE.SYS.

If you are using SPSSPC+, remember that you have a choice about what disc and directory the system file ends up on. As noted in Chapter 2, I have assumed that EXAMPLE.DAT was saved on a disc situated in the A: drive. I will assume that you also want to put your system file on a disc in the A: drive. The command for this would be:

*spss/pc:*SAVE OUTFILE='A:EXAMPLE.SYS'.

Compressing system files

SPSS system files are often quite a bit larger than the ASCII files from which they were originally derived. This is because each number is normally stored in a space which is large enough to hold a number with at least eight significant digits. If your data are mainly integers (whole numbers), then you can **compress** your system file when you save it and save a great deal of space. The only disadvantage of doing this is that retrieving the system file takes the computer a little longer (not much).

To save a compressed system file you simply put /COMPRESS at the end of the save command. Thus you could have typed in:

spss-x> SAVE OUTFILE=EXAMPLE.SYS /COMPRESS.

Retrieving system files

If you were to exit from SPSS at this point and then go back into it at some other time, you could restore the workspace that was saved by typing the command:

spss-x> GET FILE=EXAMPLE.SYS.

This GET command is used **instead of** the DATA LIST command.

If you are using SPSSPC+, and have saved the system file on the A: drive, you type:

```
SPSS/PC:GET FILE='A:EXAMPLE.SYS'.
```

Note: The original data file, EXAMPLE.DAT, will still be on your disc, but you probably will not need it again unless you find some error in the data and need to change EXAMPLE.DAT and read in the revised version.

Once the workspace has been saved in a file (e.g. EXAMPLE.SYS), you do not need to save it again, unless you carry out some transformations on the data which you want to keep. The system file will sit there on your disc ready for you to use until you delete it.

When to save SPSS system files

You can save the workspace as many times as you like during a session. For example, you may save it once as soon as you have read the data in using the DATA LIST command. You can save it again once you have recoded the missing data, and again once you have carried out some compute commands. Obviously, there is only any point in saving a new system file if the workspace has been changed in some way since the last time the system file was saved. If you try to save a system file using the same name as one you have used before, SPSS may tell you that you cannot do it. This is to stop people accidentally overwriting one system file with another when in fact they still wanted to keep the first one as well.

Any changes to the workspace (using RECODE, COMPUTE, IF, or SELECT IF commands) carried out after you have saved a system file will **not** be saved unless you use the SAVE command again to save the new version of the workspace.

You can only use the GET command to read in a worksheet which has been saved using the SAVE command. Do not try to use GET to read in data from an ASCII data file. In that case you use the DATA LIST command as described in' Chapter 2.

I tend to use the suffix SYS in the file name to denote a system file (e.g. EXAMPLE.SYS) but of course you can use any name you like.

4.2 Saving and restoring MINITAB system files

The principles underlying the use of MINITAB system files are exactly the same as those for SPSS system files (see above).

Saving system files
Suppose that you had gone into MINITAB and read in EXAMPLE.DAT using the READ command. You could then save the workspace containing that data using the command:

MTB>   SAVE 'EXAMPLE.MTB'

If you were using the PC version of MINITAB and wanted to save the system file on a disc in the A: drive, you would type:

MTB>   SAVE 'A:EXAMPLE.MTB'

Retrieving system files
You could then finish the MINITAB session and at some later date go back into MINITAB and type the command:

MTB>   RETRIEVE 'EXAMPLE.MTB'

or if you were using the PC version and had saved the system file on a disc in the A: drive:

MTB>   RETRIEVE 'A:EXAMPLE.MTB'

This restores the workspace exactly as it was when you saved EXAMPLE.MTB.

Remember, the RETRIEVE command is used **instead of** the READ command.

When to save MINITAB system files

You can save the workspace as many times as you like during a session. For example, you may save it once as soon as you have read the data in using the READ command. You can save it again once you have recoded the missing data, and again once you have carried out some compute commands. Obviously, there is only any point in saving a new system file if the workspace has been changed in some way since the last time the system file was saved.

Any changes to the workspace (using CODE, COPY or LET commands) carried out after you have saved a system file will **not** be saved unless you use the SAVE command again to save the new version of the workspace.

You can only use the RETRIEVE command to read in a worksheet which has been save using the SAVE command. Do not try to use RETRIEVE to read in data from an ASCII data file. In that case you use the READ command as described in Chapter 2.

I use the suffix MTB in the file name to denote a MINITAB system file (e.g. EXAMPLE.MTB) but of course you can use any name you like.

4.3 Conclusion

You should now know how to avoid having to read the raw data in and perform transformations every time you want to analyze a data set. You use the SAVE command at the point when you want to take a snapshot of the workspace, then at some later date you can use the GET (for SPSS) or RETRIEVE (for MINITAB) command to restore the workspace to how it was when you saved it.

Chapter 5

Means, standard deviations and other descriptive statistics

You should by now be able to:

- create an ASCII data file using a text editor
- begin an SPSS or MINITAB session on the computer
- read data from a data file into the MINITAB or SPSS workspace
- carry out any necessary transformations to data in the SPSS workspace including recoding missing values
- save and restore SPSS or MINITAB system files

The remainder of this book shows how to use SPSS and MINITAB to calculate statistics ranging from the simplest frequency data, to complex multivariate analyses.

This chapter shows how to calculate simple, quantitative, descriptive statistics from your data.

Note: You should always obtain descriptive statistics on your data of the kind mentioned in this chapter and in Chapter 6 before going on to further analyses. You may pick up errors in the data file which you had not previously spotted.

5.1 Descriptive statistics in SPSS

Before you start
The examples in this chapter and all the remaining chapters

assume that you have created the data file EXAMPLE.DAT, and that you are in an SPSS session with the data loaded into the workspace and the missing values recoded. You should have done the following at least once.

```
$        SPSSX   (To get into SPSS-X)
SPSS-X> DATA LIST FILE=EXAMPLE.DAT FREE / SUBNO CRAV1
CONT>    DIFF1 CRAV2 DIFF2 CRAV3 DIFF3 CRAV4 DIFF4 SEX
CONT>    COND AGE CO PSY HAND INDUL SED STIM AUTO
CONT>    ADD DEPEND CIGSPD MOTIV TROUB.
SPSS-X> MISSING VALUES CRAV1 TO DIFF4 SEX (9) AGE CO
CONT>    CIGSPD (99).
SPSS-X> SAVE OUTFILE=EXAMPLE.SYS.
```

In SPSSPC+ the corresponding commands would be:

```
c:\>     SPSSPC
SPSS/PC:DATA LIST FILE='A:EXAMPLE.DAT' FREE / SUBNO
CONT>    CRAV1 DIFF1 CRAV2 DIFF2 CRAV3 DIFF3 CRAV4
CONT>    DIFF4 SEX COND AGE CO PSY HAND INDUL SED STIM
CONT>    AUTO ADD DEPEND CIGSPD MOTIV TROUB.
SPSS/PC:MISSING VALUES CRAV1 TO DIFF4 SEX (9) AGE CO
CONT>    CIGSPD (99).
CONT>    SAVE OUTFILE='A:EXAMPLE.SYS'.
```

After you have executed these commands once, every time you begin a new session you can simply type the command:

```
SPSS-X> GET FILE=EXAMPLE.SYS.
```

in the case of SPSS-X, or

```
SPSS/PC:GET FILE='A:EXAMPLE.SYS'.
```

if you are using SPSSPC+.

Simple quantitative statistics

To obtain the means and standard deviations (SDs) of the variables, CRAV1, CRAV2 CRAV3 and CRAV4, you would type:

```
SPSS-X> DESCR VAR=CRAV1 CRAV2 CRAV3 CRAV4.
```

The only thing you would need to change for your own data is the list of variables you want to obtain descriptive statistics on.

When you execute this command, SPSS produces a display of which the relevant part is as follows:

```
Number of Valid Observations (Listwise) =        56.00

Variable      Mean    Std Dev  Minimum   Maximum    N  Label
CRAV1         2.96      1.56     1.00      6.00      56
CRAV2         2.61      1.30     1.00      5.00      56
CRAV3         2.30      1.22     1.00      6.00      56
CRAV4         1.59       .60     1.00      3.00      56
```

To get the means and SDs of these variables broken down by SEX, you type the command:

SPSS-X> MEANS CRAV1 CRAV2 CRAV3 CRAV4 BY SEX.

The display produced by this command is shown below for the variable CRAV4 only. You should find it self-explanatory. Similar output is given for each variable on the variable list (e.g. CRAV1, CRAV2 etc.).

```
Criterion Variable    CRAV4
    Broken Down by    SEX

Variable       Value  Label              Mean    Std Dev   Cases
For Entire Population                    1.5893    .5963      56
SEX             1.00                     1.5357    .5762      28
SEX             2.00                     1.6429    .6215      28

Total Cases = 56
```

The variable used to classify the subjects (in this case SEX) must have integer values such as 1 for females and 2 for males.

Note: In this output, as in many others, there will be a column called "LABEL" which has nothing in it. This is for situations where you have assigned labels to values of your variables to help remind you what they represent. I have not covered this feature in this book.

You can obtain your means and SDs broken down by more than one variable. For example, to obtain a break down of means and SDs by both SEX and COND, you would type the command:

```
SPSS-X>  MEANS CRAV1 CRAV2 CRAV3 CRAV4 BY SEX BY
CONT>    COND.
```

To obtain the median of a set of variables, you use the FREQ command. For example, to obtain the median of CRAV1, CRAV2, CRAV3 and CRAV4, you type:

```
SPSS-X>  FREQ VAR=CRAV1 CRAV2 CRAV3 CRAV4 / STAT =
CONT>    MEDIAN.
```

Obtaining the medians separately for subgroups of cases is more tricky. The way to do it is to use the TEMPORARY and SELECT IF commands (or the PROCESS IF command if you are using SPSSPC+) to pick out those cases, and then use the FREQ command.

Thus to obtain the medians broken down by SEX, you could have:

```
SPSS-X>  TEMPORARY.
SPSS-X>  SELECT IF (SEX=1).
SPSS-X>  FREQ VAR=CRAV1 CRAV2 CRAV3 CRAV4 / STAT =
CONT>    MEDIAN.
SPSS-X>  TEMPORARY.
SPSS-X>  SELECT IF (SEX=2).
SPSS-X>  FREQ VAR=CRAV1 CRAV2 CRAV3 CRAV4 / STAT =
CONT>    MEDIAN.
```

This will select the females first and then get their median values. It will then select the males and do the same thing.

Note: You must use the TEMPORARY command otherwise when you select the females, the males will be lost from the workspace and you will have to retrieve the data file or system file where all the data were kept (see Chapter 4).

When using SPSSPC+, you substitute the single command
PROCESS IF for the TEMPORARY and SELECT IF
commands. See Chapter 3.

5.2 Descriptive statistics in MINITAB

Before you begin
This chapter assumes that in this session of MINITAB you
have the data from EXAMPLE.DAT in the workspace, with
missing values already recoded. You should execute these
commands at least once.

```
$        MINITAB
MTB>     READ 'EXAMPLE.DAT' C1-C24
MTB>     CODE (9) '*' C2-C12 C2-C12
MTB>     CODE (99) '*' C12 C13 C22 C12 C13 C22
MTB>     SAVE 'EXAMPLE.MTB'
```

The corresponding commands for the PC version of MINITAB
are:

```
c:\>     MINITAB
MTB>     READ 'A:EXAMPLE.DAT' C1-C24
MTB>     CODE (9) '*' C2-C12 C2-C12
MTB>     CODE (99) '*' C12 C13 C22 C12 C13 C22
MTB>     SAVE 'A:EXAMPLE.MTB'
```

After you have executed these commands once, every time you
begin a new session you can simply type the command:

RETR 'EXAMPLE.MTB'

if you are using the mainframe, or

RETR 'A:EXAMPLE.MTB'

if you are using the PC version of MINITAB.

Simple quantitative statistics
To get the means and SDs of the four craving scores (C2, C4,
C6 and C8) in EXAMPLE.DAT, type:

```
MTB>     DESCR C2 C4 C6 C8
```

This is very similar to the SPSS command. Only the variable names and the lack of a full stop at the end are different.

The output is given below. Notice that you also get the median, standard error of the mean (SD divided by square root of the number of cases), maximum, minimum, and first and third quartiles. You may also notice that the presentation is much more concise than that of SPSS.

```
             N      MEAN    MEDIAN    TRMEAN    STDEV    SEMEAN
C2          56     2.964     3.000     2.900    1.560     0.209
C4          56     2.607     2.500     2.560    1.303     0.174
C6          56     2.304     2.000     2.200    1.220     0.163
C8          56    1.5893    2.0000    1.5400   0.5963    0.0797

           MIN       MAX        Q1        Q3
C2       1.000     6.000     2.000     4.000
C4       1.000     5.000     1.250     3.750
C6       1.000     6.000     1.000     3.000
C8      1.0000    3.0000    1.0000    2.0000
```

To get means and SDs of these variables broken down by sex (C10), type:

```
MTB>    TABLES C10;
SUBC>   STATS C2 C4 C6 C8.
```

Remember to press the Enter key after the semicolon - this will produce the prompt SUBC> (meaning that MINITAB is waiting for a subcommand) in response to which you type the STATS C2 C4 C6 C8.

Note: Do not forget the full stop after C8. Whenever you type in a subcommand you must tell MINITAB that you have finished by using a full stop.

```
ROWS: C10

        C2      C2        C2     C4      C4      C4    C6        C6
        N      MEAN    STD DEV    N     MEAN   STD DEV  N       MEAN

  1     28    2.7143    1.3294    28   2.5357  1.3467  28     2.1429
  2     28    3.2143    1.7503    28   2.6786  1.2781  28     2.4643
ALL     56    2.9643    1.5605    56   2.6071  1.3028  56     2.3036

            C6      C8        C8       C8
        STD DEV     N       MEAN    STD DEV

  1     1.2387     28      1.5357    0.5762
  2     1.2015     28      1.6429    0.6215
ALL     1.2198     56      1.5893    0.5963
```

The results of this command are shown above. The row labelled 1 gives the statistics for Group 1 (females) and row 2 refers to Group 2 (males).

You can obtain your means and SDs broken down by more than one variable. For example, to obtain a breakdown of means and SDs by both sex (C10) and condition (C11), you would type the command:

```
MTB>    TABLE C10 BY C11;
SUBC>   STATS C2 C4 C6 C8.
```

To obtain the medians of separate subgroups, you can use the TABLE command as follows:

```
MTB>    TABLE C10 BY C11;
SUBC>   MEDIAN C2 C4 C6 C8.
```

5.3 Conclusion

You should now be able to obtain simple quantitative descriptive statistics from your data. You can perhaps begin to see the enormous saving in time and effort that can be achieved by using a statistics package. A single command of one or two lines can take the place of several hours work calculating statistics on a large number of variables. What is more, the computer will always get it right.

Chapter 6

Frequencies, proportions and histograms

You will often need to find out how many cases fall into various categories. For example, you may wish to obtain the number and proportion of males and females in a sample. Both SPSS and MINITAB have simple commands for doing this, and they can also provide crude histograms so that you can look at the distribution of your data (for example, to see whether it approximates a normal distribution).

Note: You should check on the distributions of your variables before carrying out further analyses on them. Apart from influencing your choice of statistical test (see later chapters), it will help you pick up errors in the data file which you might not have spotted before. For example, the 24 hour craving scores should all be between 1 and 6 so if you spot any values higher than 6 you will know that an error has occurred when typing in the data.

6.1 Frequencies, proportions and histograms in SPSS

The examples in this chapter assume that you have begun an SPSS session and have the data from EXAMPLE.DAT in your current workspace, with missing values already recoded. See the beginning of Chapter 5 if you are in doubt about how to do this.

Suppose you wished to know how many males and females there were in the sample, also how many subjects there were in each condition. You would type the command:

```
SPSS-X> FREQ VAR=SEX COND.
```

This would also give the proportions falling into the two categories. The main part of the SPSS output arising from this command is given below just for the variable SEX. It makes it apparent that there are 28 cases (50% of the sample) with the value 1 (females) and 28 cases with value 2 (males). Valid percent refers to the percent of cases with each value once missing values have been excluded.

SEX

Value	Frequency	Percent	Valid Percent	Cum Percent
1.00	28	50.0	50.0	50.0
2.00	28	50.0	50.0	100.0
TOTAL	56	100.0	100.0	

The only thing you need to change for your own data is the list of variables. You can specify as many variables as you like. You can, as with any list of variables in SPSS, use the word **TO** to indicate a whole range of variables without spelling each one out individually.

Thus you could have:

```
SPSS-X> FREQ VAR=CRAV1 TO DIFF4.
```

which would give frequencies for CRAV1, DIFF1, CRAV2, DIFF2, CRAV3, DIFF3, CRAV4 and DIFF4.

The frequencies are worked out separately for each variable which you specify.

If you wished to see histograms representing the data graphically you could use:

```
SPSS-X> FREQ VAR=CRAV1 TO DIFF1/FORMAT=NOTABLE/HIST.
```

The subcommand /FORMAT=NOTABLE stops it printing out

all the frequencies as well in a separate table. Here is the kind of output you can expect from this command. In addition to giving a graphical representation of the frequency of each value it provides a frequency count down the left hand side.

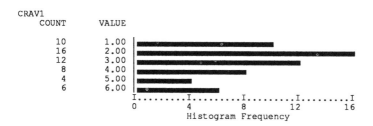

```
CRAV1
      COUNT        VALUE
         10         1.00
         16         2.00
         12         3.00
          8         4.00
          4         5.00
          6         6.00
                          I.........I.........I.........I.........I
                          0        4        8       12       16
                               Histogram Frequency
```

Note: If the variable for which you want a histogram includes a wide range of values and/or non-integer data, SPSS will automatically aggregate values into **bins** for the purposes of presentation. It will not necessarily give the frequencies of each value individually.

Multi-way classification

To find out the numbers of subjects falling into each cell of a multi-way classification, say of SEX by MOTIV, you use the CROSS command, as in:

SPSS-X> CROSS SEX BY MOTIV.

You would usually want proportions and a test of the statistical significance of any association between the two variables. In that case use:

SPSS-X> CROSS SEX BY MOTIV / CELLS=ROW COLUMN / STATS=CHIS.

SPSSPC+ users have a slightly different command:

*SPSS/PC:*CROSS SEX BY MOTIV / OPTIONS=3 4 /STATS=1.

This will provide both the row-wise and the column-wise

percentage of subjects in each cell. Sometimes, it makes sense to express the percentages one way and sometimes another. Here is an example of the kind of output that is obtained:

```
SEX  by  MOTIV

                    MOTIV
            Row Pct |
            Col Pct |
                    |                                              Row
                    |   2.00|   3.00|   4.00|   5.00|   6.00| Total
SEX         --------+-------+-------+-------+-------+-------+
            1.00  |  14.3  |  10.7  |  46.4  |  17.9  |   7.1  |    28
                  |  57.1  |  75.0  |  43.3  |  71.4  |  40.0  |  50.0
                  +--------+--------+--------+--------+--------+
            2.00  |  10.7  |   3.6  |  60.7  |   7.1  |  10.7  |    28
                  |  42.9  |  25.0  |  56.7  |  28.6  |  60.0  |  50.0
                  +--------+--------+--------+--------+--------+
          Column      7        4        30       7        5       56
(Continued) Total    12.5      7.1     53.6     12.5      8.9    100.0

                    MOTIV
            Row Pct |
            Col Pct |
                    |           Row
                    |   7.00| Total
SEX         --------+-------+
            1.00  |   3.6  |    28
                  |  33.3  |  50.0
                  +--------+
            2.00  |   7.1  |    28
                  |  66.7  |  50.0
                  +--------+
          Column      3        56
          Total      5.4     100.0
```

Chi-Square	Value	DF
Pearson	3.49524	5
Likelihood Ratio	3.59421	5
Mantel-Haenszel	.41667	1

Minimum Expected Frequency -   1.500
Cells with Expected Frequency < 5 -   10 OF   12 (83.3%)

Notice that the first mentioned variable in the CROSS command (SEX in this case), becomes the rows and the second becomes the columns. Thus the top left cell row percentage is the percentage of males (14.3) who report that social reasons (category 2 in the variable, MOTIV) are their most important motives for smoking. The top left cell column percentage is the proportion of subjects with social smoking motives who are male (57.1).

If you only want the row-wise percentages leave out the word COLUMN (or the number 4 after OPTIONS in SPSSPC+). If you only want the column-wise percentages leave out the word ROW (or the number 3 in SPSSPC+).

In fact there were no cases falling into category 1 of the smoking motivation variable (MOTIV), so this column is omitted by SPSS.

Note: The CROSS command can only be used with integer variables (variables containing whole numbers).

You are given a range of Chi-square statistics to choose from. In general, you can use the Pearson. The output shown above was generated by SPSS-X. The SPSSPC+ output only gives one Chi-square statistic. To assess whether there association between the variables is statistically significant you have to look up the Chi-square statistic in your statistical tables.

In the example used here, the SPSS output tells us that a large proportion of the cells in the frequency table had expected frequencies of less than 5. This is a useful diagnostic device because Chi-square tests are based on the assumption that most of the cells will have expected frequencies larger than this. It would be prudent in this case, therefore, to collapse across or omit categories with few subjects in, or better still, increase the sample size.

When you have a two-by-two table, you are offered Chi-square statistics with Yates correction and without. Yates correction should normally be used.

With two-by-two tables and very small sample sizes, SPSS calculates a Fisher's exact probability instead of using Chi-square.

When you already have frequency data
Sometimes your raw data is already in the form of frequency

counts and you do not want to have to enter it subject by subject. You may want to perform a Chi-square test on this data nevertheless. Suppose for example you have the following data:

```
Number of male smokers: 52
Number of female smokers: 21
Number of male non-smokers: 54
Number of female non-smokers: 70
```

There are 197 subjects represented here and you do not want to enter the data for each one individually! You can create a data file (call it EXAMPLE2.DAT) with just the following data in it:

```
1 1 52
1 2 21
2 1 54
2 2 70
```

The first variable which we will call SMOKE is whether or not the subject is a smoker (1=smoker, 2=non-smoker); the second variable is sex (1=males, 2=females); the third variable is the number of subjects in each category. Thus there are 52 male smokers, 21 females smokers, and so on.

You should follow the instructions in Appendix 1 or 2 to create the file, or consult your computer centre.

Your SPSS commands to get the proportions in each cell and the Chi-square statistic assessing the extent to which smoking is associated with gender would be:

```
SPSS-X> DATA LIST FILE=EXAMPLE2.DAT FREE/SMOKE SEX
CONT>    NUMBER.
SPSS-X> WEIGHT BY NUMBER.
SPSS-X> CROSS SMOKE BY SEX/CELLS=ROW COLUMN / STATS = CHISQ.
```

For SPSSPC+ users the commands are:

```
SPSS/PC:DATA LIST FILE='A:EXAMPLE2.DAT' FREE/SMOKE SEX
CONT>    NUMBER.
SPSS/PC:WEIGHT BY NUMBER.
SPSS/PC:CROSS SMOKE BY SEX/OPT=3 4/STATS=1.
```

You use the WEIGHT command to tell SPSS that the variable

you have called NUMBER is to be treated as a set of frequencies.

Log-linear models with multi-way frequency tables

There are occasions when one would like to examine relationships between more than two categorical variables. For example, in EXAMPLE.DAT we may wish to know whether there is an association between the smokers' most important self-reported smoking motive (MOTIV) and what they consider to be the most troublesome withdrawal symptom (TROUB) as a function of what condition they were in (COND).

Simple Chi-square tests will not suffice for this analysis because more than two variables are involved. It is analogous to the need for analysis of variance rather than t-tests when comparing scores on numeric variables with more than one independent variable.

The analysis required is log-linear modelling of the frequency tables. There are many facets of this technique but I will concentrate on the simple identification of statistically significant associations between categories of variables. Suppose that you wished to know whether there was an association between the most troublesome withdrawal symptom (TROUB) and most important smoking motive (MOTIV), taking account of sex (SEX), you would type the command:

```
SPSS-X>  HILOGLIN TROUB (1,4) MOTIV (2,7) SEX (1,2) /
CONT>    PRINT=ASSOC.
```

The only things you need to change for your own analyses are the variable names (e.g. TROUB, MOTIV), and the numbers in brackets after each one. These indicate the maximum and minimum values that each variable can take. Thus TROUB can take on values between 1 and 4 and MOTIV can take on values between 2 and 7. (There are no subjects with value 1.) Only integers are allowed.

Here is the main part of the output from this command:

```
The Iterative Proportional Fit algorithm converged at iteration 1.
The maximum difference between observed and fitted marginal totals is
.000 and the convergence criterion is      .250

Goodness-of-fit test statistics

        Likelihood ratio chi square =       .00000   DF = 0  P = 1.000
                   Pearson chi square =       .00000   DF = 0  P = 1.000

Tests that K-way and higher order effects are zero.

    K    DF    L.R. Chisq   Prob   Pearson Chisq    Prob   Iteration

    3    15      11.308    .7305      10.101       .8134        3
    2    38      51.781    .0672      69.092       .0015        2
    1    47     114.803    .0000     190.857       .0000        0


Tests that K-way effects are zero.

    K    DF    L.R. Chisq   Prob   Pearson Chisq    Prob   Iteration

    1     9      63.022    .0000     121.765       .0000        0
    2    23      40.474    .0136      58.992       .0001        0
    3    15      11.308    .7305      10.101       .8134        0

NOTE    13865
DF used for tests have NOT been adjusted for structural or sampling zeros in
HILOG OR LOGLIN.  Tests using these DF may be conservative.



Tests of PARTIAL associations.

Effect Name                    DF   Partial Chisq    Prob  Iter

TROUB*MOTIV                    15      30.750       .0095    2
TROUB*SEX                       3       5.194       .1581    2
MOTIV*SEX                       5       2.658       .7525    2
TROUB                           3      20.850       .0001    2
MOTIV                           5      42.171       .0000    2
SEX                             1        .000      1.0000    2
```

The goodness-of-fit test statistics mean nothing in this context and should be ignored. The significance of the 3-way association between TROUB, MOTIV and SEX is given in the table which is headed "Tests that K-way effects are zero". The last line of that table, where K is 3, has a Pearson Chi-square statistic of 10.101 with 15 degrees of freedom. The probability of this occurring by chance given no association between the three variables is .8134 which is NOT less than the .05 figure normally required for statistical significance. Thus there is no significant 3-way association.

To see whether there are any significant 2-way associations,

taking account of values on the third variable, look at the table headed "Tests of PARTIAL associations". The Chi-square statistics for the association between TROUB and MOTIV, taking account of SEX, is 30.750 with 15 degrees of freedom. The probability of getting this by chance is .0095 which is less than .05 and therefore we can say that there is a statistically significant association between the most troublesome withdrawal symptom and most important motive for smoking, taking account of any sex differences. The absence of a 3-way interaction indicates that there is no evidence that this association is different for males and females.

No other 2-way interactions were significant.

You may notice that there is a NOTE 13865 which states that the degrees of freedom in the tests of partial associations have not been adjusted for the fact that there might be no cases in one or more of the cells of the frequency table. In this example there were some cells with either no or very few subjects in. This would make the test conservative (less likely than it should be to indicate a significant association). If you get this warning, you may want to combine some categories to boost the numbers in certain cells, or omit certain categories with very few cases in from the analysis.

6.2 Frequencies, proportions and histograms in MINITAB

The examples in this chapter assume that you are currently in a MINITAB session and your workspace contains the data from EXAMPLE.DAT, with missing values recoded. See Chapter 5 for the necessary commands if you are still unsure how to do this.

If you want to know how many males and females (C10) there were in the sample represented by EXAMPLE.DAT, you would type the command:

MTB>   TALLY C10

This just gives a count of how many cases fall into each

category. To get this expressed as percentages, you have to use the subcommand PERCENT, as in:

```
MTB>    TALLY C10;
SUBC>   PERCENT.
```

You can get frequency data of this kind for several variables at a time. So if you wanted to find out the percentages of cases in each condition (C11) as well, you would type:

```
MTB>    TALLY C10 C11;
SUBC>   PERCENT.
```

If you wished to see histograms representing the number of cases with different levels of craving after 24 hours, one could use:

```
MTB>    HIST C2
```

You can specify more than one variable. The histograms will appear one after the other for each variable mentioned. Here is the kind of output you can expect:

```
Histogram of C2   N = 56

Midpoint    Count
       1       10   **********
       2       16   ****************
       3       12   ************
       4        8   ********
       5        4   ****
       6        6   ******
```

To find out the numbers of subjects falling into each cell of a multi-way classification, say of most important motive for smoking (C23) and most troublesome withdrawal symptom (C24), you use the TABLE command, as in:

```
MTB>    TABLE C23 BY C24;
SUBC>   COLPERCENTS;
SUBC>   CHISQ.
```

This will give the column-wise percentages of subjects in each cell of the two-way classification. If you do not have the COLPERCENTS subcommand you will get just a count of the cases in each cell. The CHISQ subcommand tells MINITAB to perform a Chi-square test on the association between the two variables.

```
ROWS: C23      COLUMNS: C24

              1        2        3        4       ALL

2            --     14.29    28.57      --      12.50
              0        3        4        0         7

3           5.26     4.76    14.29      --       7.14
              1        1        2        0         4

4          89.47    42.86    28.57      --      53.57
             17        9        4        0        30

5           5.26     9.52    14.29   100.00    12.50
              1        2        2        2         7

6            --     19.05     7.14      --       8.93
              0        4        1        0         5

7            --      9.52     7.14      --       5.36
              0        2        1        0         3

ALL       100.00   100.00   100.00   100.00   100.00
             19       21       14        2        56

CHI-SQUARE =      34.154    WITH D.F. =    15

CELL CONTENTS --
                  % OF COL
                  COUNT
```

The output that is obtained is given above. Notice that the first mentioned variable in the TABLE command (C23 in this case), becomes the rows and the second (C24) forms the columns. The upper number in each cell is the columnwise percentage and the lower number is the actual frequency.

Notice that MINITAB does not tell you whether your Chi-square statistic indicated a significant association or not. You will have to look it up in your statistical tables. Importantly, neither does MINITAB tell you whether the assumptions of the Chi-square test (in terms of the need for a minimum expected in frequency in most cells) have been violated. In this case, they were violated because there were a large number of cells for a relatively small sample size.

When you already have frequency data

Sometimes your raw data is already in the form of frequency counts and you do not want to have to enter it subject by subject. You may want to perform a Chi-square test on this data nevertheless. Suppose for example you have the following data:

```
Number of male smokers: 52
Number of female smokers: 21
Number of male non-smokers: 54
Number of female non-smokers: 70
```

There are 197 subjects represented here and you do not want to enter the data for each one individually! You can set up a data file (call it EXAMPLE2.DAT) with just the following data in it (this is done using an editor as described in Appendix 1):

```
1 1 52
1 2 21
2 1 54
2 2 70
```

Your MINITAB commands to get the proportions in each cell and the Chi-square statistic assessing the extent to which smoking is associated with gender would be:

```
MTB>     READ 'EXAMPLE2.DAT' C1-C3
MTB>     TABLE C1 BY C2;
SUBC>    FREQUENCIES C3;
SUBC>    COLPERCENTS;
SUBC>    CHISQ.
```

Note: In this example we had three subcommands. MINITAB allows several subcommands at a time; you put a semi-colon at the end of each one to tell that another one is coming.

The subcommand COLPERCENTS was put in so that the cells would contain column-wise percentages and not just the number of cases in the cell.

6.3 Conclusion

This chapter has explained how to obtain information on the frequencies and proportions of cases falling into particular categories. For many researchers, this is all they ever need to know. You have also been told how to obtain a Chi-square statistic to assess the statistical significance of an association between categorical variables (variables consisting of categories to which cases can either belong or not). The next chapter examines how to obtain associations between quantitative variables (ones which cases can be given a number on, e.g. reaction times, ratings, age, IQ).

Chapter 7

Correlations and scatter plots

7.1 Correlations

If you have recorded quantitative data from a group of subjects, you may wish to see how closely different variables relate to each other. For example, you may wish to see whether subjects with faster visual reaction times also tend to have faster auditory reaction times.

The most commonly used measure of a linear (straight line) association between two variables is Pearson's Product Moment Correlation Coefficient (**R**). If the relationship you are looking for is **monotonic** (i.e. a higher score on one variable is associated with a higher score on another) but not necessarily a straight line, you could use Spearman's Rho (**r**). If you are looking for a monotonic relationship between two variables and at least one of them can only take on a small number of values (e.g. high, medium and low), you should probably use Kendall's Tau **b**.

Values of R, r and Tau b can lie between 1 and -1. A value of 1 means a perfect positive association (the two variables go up and down together); a value of 0 means there is no association of any kind; a value of -1 means that there is a perfect negative association (as one goes up the other goes down).

SPSS-X and SPSSPC+ provides R, r and Tau b. MINITAB provides R and r.

Calculating R and r in SPSS
This chapter assumes that you are in SPSS with data from EXAMPLE.DAT loaded into the workspace and missing values

recoded. See the beginning of Chapter 5 for the necessary commands if you are unsure.

To obtain the Pearson correlation coefficient between two variables you use the command CORR followed by the variable names.

Suppose, for example, that you wished to see how closely the cigarette dependence score (DEPEND) was associated with the number of cigarettes smoked per day (CIGSPD), you would type the command:

SPSS-X> CORR DEPEND CIGSPD.

You might wish to see correlations between several pairs of variables. For example, suppose that you wished to examine the correlations between CRAV1, CRAV2, CRAV3 and CRAV4. You could type:

SPSS-X> CORR CRAV1 CRAV2 CRAV3 CRAV4.

This command gives correlations between all the possible pairings of these variables as shown below.

```
- - - -  P E A R S O N   C O R R E L A T I O N   C O E F F I C I E N T S  -

            CRAV1        CRAV2        CRAV3        CRAV4

CRAV1       1.0000        .8426        .7986        .0426
           (   56)      (   56)      (   56)      (   56)
           P= .         P= .000      P= .000      P= .378

CRAV2        .8426       1.0000        .7400       -.0242
           (   56)      (   56)      (   56)      (   56)
           P= .000      P= .         P= .000      P= .430

CRAV3        .7986        .7400       1.0000        .1245
           (   56)      (   56)      (   56)      (   56)
           P= .000      P= .000      P= .         P= .180

CRAV4        .0426       -.0242        .1245       1.0000
           (   56)      (   56)      (   56)      (   56)
           P= .378      P= .430      P= .180      P= .

(COEFFICIENT / (CASES) / 1-TAILED SIG)

" . " IS PRINTED IF A COEFFICIENT CANNOT BE COMPUTED
```

The set of correlations produced is known as a **correlation**

matrix. Below each correlation is a figure in brackets - this is the number of subjects used in that correlation. The figure below that is the significance level - it should be less than .05 for you to be able to say that the correlation is significantly different from 0. Notice that the test used in **one-tailed**.

Note: A one-tailed test is appropriate only if you have prior reason to expect that any correlation you found would be in a particular direction (e.g. positive).

If you want a two-tailed test you can either double the p values yourself (p=.035 becomes p=.070), or you can set an option in the command as follows:

SPSS-X> CORR CRAV1 TO DIFF4 / PRINT=TWOTAIL.

In this example the variables are specified as CRAV1 TO DIFF4. This tells SPSS to include all the variables located between CRAV1 and DIFF4 in the analysis. These are: CRAV1, DIFF1, CRAV2, DIFF2, CRAV3, DIFF3, CRAV4 and DIFF4 (see the DATA LIST command in Chapter 2 which was used to read the data into the SPSS workspace).

To get the same result, SPSSPC+ users have the following command:

*SPSS/PC:*CORR CRAV1 TO DIFF4/OPT=3 5.

OPT=3 5 indicates that a two-tailed significance test is to be used (Option 3), and that SPSS is to display the exact significance level of the correlation (Option 5).

If you do not specify Option 5 you will just see that some of the correlations are marked with an asterisk in the screen display. A single asterisk indicates that the correlation is significant at p<.01; a double asterisk indicates that p<.001.

Given that most psychologists use a significance level of p<.05, these asterisks are not all that useful and Option 5 is almost always needed.

When you have missing values on some variables, and you do not tell SPSS any different, it will leave out the whole case, including all its variables (missing or otherwise), from the analysis. This is wasteful because there may be other correlations in the matrix which have no missing values in the variables concerned. You therefore want SPSS only to omit cases with missing values when the actual variables used in any given correlation have missing values.

To do this you use the option, /MISSING = PAIRWISE, for SPSS-X users, and /OPT=2 for SPSSPC+ users. Thus the commands used above would look like this:

```
SPSS-X> CORR CRAV1 TO DIFF4 / PRINT=TWOTAIL / MISSING=
CONT>    PAIRWISE.

SPSS/PC:CORR CRAV1 TO DIFF4 / OPT=2 3 5.
```

If you have had difficulty in understanding what to do and when, just remember to use these last versions of the command - they give you all the results you are likely to need.

To obtain Spearman correlations for CRAV1 to DIFF4, type:

```
SPSS-X> NONPAR CORR CRAV1 TO DIFF4 / PRINT = TWOTAIL
CONT>    / MISSING = PAIRWISE.
```

To obtain Spearman's r using SPSSPC+, you first create new variables which contain the **ranks** of the original variables. Then you calculate the Pearson's R on the ranks.

Thus if you want to calculate the r for dependence (DEPEND) and cigarettes per day (CIGSPD), you do the following:

```
SPSS/PC:RANK DEPEND BY DEPEND.
SPSS/PC:RANK CIGSPD BY CIGSPD.
SPSS/PC:CORR RDEPEND RCIGSPD / OPT=2 3 5.
```

The first RANK command takes the variable DEPEND, and produces a new variable which SPSSPC+ automatically calls RDEPEND (standing for "Rank of DEPEND") containing the rank ordering of values in it. The lowest value gets a value of 1; the next lowest gets a value of 2. Sometimes, two or more cases have the same value; they are **tied**. Each tied value receives the average rank of all those with which it is tied.

The second RANK command does the same for CIGSPD. Then the CORR command calculates a Pearson's R on the new ranked variables.

When your sample size is reasonably large (above 30) you can use the significance levels provided by SPSSPC+. When you have small samples you should ignore the SPSSPC+ significance levels and look up the statistical significance of **r** in tables of Spearman's r.

Kendall's Tau b
To calculate Tau b using SPSS-X you use NONPAR CORR as in:

```
SPSS-X>  NONPAR CORR CRAV1 TO DIFF4 / PRINT= TWOTAIL
CONT>    KENDALL / MISSING = PAIRWISE.
```

To calculate Tau b using SPSSPC+ you have to specify the pairs of variables one at a time using the CROSS command. Suppose that you want to calculate the Tau b for the relationship between CRAV1 and DIFF1, you type:

```
SPSS/PC:CROSS CRAV1 BY DIFF1 / OPT = 3 4 / STAT=6.
```

The problem with Tau b is that even with perfect associations it cannot give values of 1 or -1 unless the range of values in one variable is the same as that in the other. In SPSSPC+, Tau c can be used instead by specifying STAT=7 rather than STAT=6.

Calculating R and r in MINITAB
It is assumed that you have begun a MINITAB session and

have loaded data from EXAMPLE.DAT into the workspace, recoding missing values as necessary. See Chapter 5 for the necessary commands if you are unsure.

To obtain the Pearson correlation coefficient between two variables you use the command CORR followed by the variable names.

Suppose, for example, that you wished to see how closely the cigarette dependence score (C21) was associated with the number of cigarettes smoked per day (C22), you would type the command:

MTB>   CORR C21 C22

You may wish to see correlations between several pairs of variables. For example, suppose that you wished to examine the correlations between all the craving variables. You would type:

MTB>   CORR C2 C4 C6 C8

The correlation matrix which results from this command is shown below.

	C2	C4	C6
C4	0.843		
C6	0.799	0.740	
C8	0.043	-0.024	0.125

MINITAB does not tell you whether the correlations produced are significantly different from 0. You have to look these up in statistical tables.

If any of the variables have missing values, then correlations involving those variables are limited to cases without missing values. Other correlations not involving these variables are unaffected. In the technical jargon, there is "pairwise deletion of missing values".

D

To obtain Spearman's r using MINITAB, you first create new variables which contain the **ranks** of the original variables. Then you calculate the Pearson's R on the ranks. To find out whether the correlations are significant, you look them up in tables of Spearman's r for small sample sizes (<30). With larger samples, either use tables of Pearson's R or calculate a t-value to look up in t-tables.

Thus if you want to calculate the r for dependence (C21) and cigarettes per day (C22), you do the following:

```
MTB>    RANK C21 C25
MTB>    RANK C22 C26
MTB>    CORR C25 C26
```

The first RANK command takes the variable C21 and produces a new variable (C25) containing the rank ordering of values in it. The lowest value gets a value of 1; the next lowest gets a value of 2. Sometimes, two or more cases have the same value; they are **tied**. Each tied value receives the average rank of all those with which it is tied.

7.2 Scatter plots

Correlations provide a numerical index of the degree to which two variables are associated with each other. To obtain a visual impression, you have to get a scatter plot. Values on one variable are represented by position on the horizontal (X) axis, and values of the other variable are represented by position on the vertical (Y) axis.

Thus each case is represented by a **point** on the scatter plot which is **x units along** and **y units up**. If two variables are perfectly correlated with each other, then all the points (cases) will fall on a straight line. If the slope of the line is positive the correlation will be 1; if it is negative the correlation will be -1.

With psychological data, one rarely gets correlations of 1 or -1, thus there is likely to be some **scatter** around this line. There may still be a relationship between the variables, but there is also a certain amount of **noise**. The greater the noise, the lower the correlation. With a correlation of 0, there is nothing but noise.

You may remember that Pearson correlations provide an index of the **linear** relationship between two variables. This means that if two variables are closely related in a non-linear manner, a Pearson correlation will underestimate the extent of the relationship. A Spearman correlation should do somewhat better as long as the relationship is monotonic. A scatter plot can give a good indication of whether a Pearson correlation is appropriate by showing whether the relationship is basically linear or not.

Scatter Plots in SPSS

To obtain a scatter plot between two variables, say DEPEND and CIGSPD, you use the command PLOT, as in:

```
SPSS-X> PLOT PLOT=CIGSPD WITH DEPEND.
```

As shown in the output below, the first variable mentioned (CIGSPD) forms the horizontal (X) axis and the other one (DEPEND) forms the vertical (Y) axis.

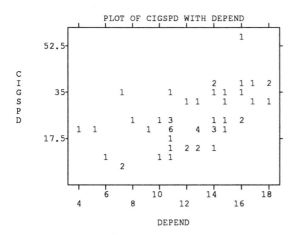

The number of subjects at each point is given (e.g. there are 6 subjects with scores on DEPEND of 11 and who smoke 18 cigs. per day. Although not shown in this example, the letters

A, B, C etc. at any given point are used to indicate that there are 10, 11, 12 etc. cases at that point.

Scatter plots in MINITAB

To obtain a scatter plot between two variables, say dependence score (C21) and cigarettes per day (C22), you type:

MTB>   PLOT C21 C22

As with SPSS the first variable mentioned becomes the X axis and the second becomes the Y axis. MINITAB scatter plots look like this:

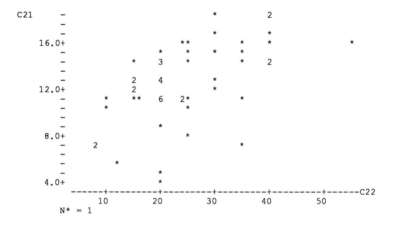

The number of subjects at each point is given (e.g. there are 6 subjects with scores on DEPEND of 11 and who smoke 18 cigs. per day. An asterisk indicates the presence of just one subject at that point.

7.3 Conclusion

This chapter has explained how to obtain simple correlations between two variables at a time. Because there are two variables involved these correlations are called **bivariate**.

Linear associations can be indexed with the Pearson's Product Moment Correlation Coefficient. This is available in both SPSS and MINITAB. Spearman's r can be used when you are only interested in assessing the extent of a monotonic relationship. To obtain r in MINITAB and SPSSPC+ you get ranks of the variables concerned and then calculate Pearson's R on the ranks. Where there are relatively few different possible values in one or both of the variables you can use Kendall's Tau b instead. This is available in SPSS-X and SPSSPC+. To examine the relationship between two variables visually, you can get scatter plots both in SPSS and MINITAB.

Chapter 8

Differences between groups

A very large part of statistical analysis in Psychology is concerned with significance testing. We saw an example of this in the previous chapter when we noted that SPSS indicates whether correlations it has calculated are significantly different from 0.

The next three chapters show you how to assess whether two or more sets of data differ from each other significantly; that is, whether the differences among them are greater than would be expected purely by chance. This chapter is concerned with testing for differences between data sets which come from different groups of individuals, for example males versus females, or a group subjected to one manipulation versus another which acts as control.

Which test to use?
If you want to compare two groups and the data are normally distributed or if the sample size is large, you use an **independent t-test**. If there are two groups and the data are not normally distributed you can use a **Mann-Whitney**. If there are more than two groups and the data are normally distributed or the sample size is large, you can use an **independent groups ANOVA**. If there are more than two groups and the data are not normally distributed you can use a **Kruskal-Wallis**.

The t-test and ANOVA are **parametric** tests. The others are **non-parametric** tests. SPSS has good facilities for carrying out all these tests. MINITAB is more restricted on the ANOVAs as we shall see.

8.1 Differences between two groups using SPSS

Suppose that you wish to determine whether the craving at 24 hours of the women in EXAMPLE.DAT is significantly different from that of the males. The command used in SPSS would be:

SPSS-X> T-TEST GROUPS = SEX(1,2) / VAR = CRAV1.

The only parts of this command that you would need to change for your own data sets are: the name of the variable specifying the groups you are comparing (in this case SEX); the part in brackets which indicates what the values of that variable are (1,2); and the name of the variable that you want to compare (in this case CRAV1).

The results of the t-test are shown below:

```
Group 1:  SEX  EQ     1.00           Group 2:  SEX  EQ     2.00

t-test for:   CRAV1
                      Number                  Standard     Standard
                     of Cases     Mean       Deviation      Error

           Group 1      28        2.7143       1.329         .251
           Group 2      28        3.2143       1.750         .331

                     | Pooled Variance Estimate | Separate Variance Estimate
      F    2-Tail    |   t    Degrees of 2-Tail |   t     Degrees of  2-Tail
   Value   Prob.     | Value   Freedom    Prob. | Value    Freedom     Prob.

    1.73    .159     | -1.20     54       .234  | -1.20     50.37       .234
```

Notice that you are given two possible t-values and their associated significance levels. One is for **pooled variance** estimates; the other is for **separate variance** estimates. To the left of the display is an **F-ratio** and an associated **significance level (2-Tail Prob.)**. To interpret the results, you have to do the following:

1. Look to see whether the significance of the F-ratio at the left of the display is less than .05. If it is, this indicates that the **variances** of the two groups you are comparing are significantly different. (This is not the same as showing that the

means are different).

2. If the variances of the two groups are significantly different you should use the significance level (2-tail Prob.) and t value under the heading **separate variances estimate**. If the variances of the two groups are not significantly different you should use the significance level under the heading **pooled variance estimate**.

The reason for this is that the pooled variance estimate assumes **homogeneity of variance** of the two groups, i.e. that the variances of the two groups you are comparing are roughly the same.

You can perform t-tests on several dependent variables using a single command simply by including a list of those variables in the list following the VAR= part of the command. For example, if you wanted to compare all the craving ratings of the males and females, you would type the command:

```
SPSS-X> T-TEST GROUPS=SEX(1,2) / VAR = CRAV1 CRAV2 CRAV3
        CRAV4.
```

Note: If you ask SPSS to carry out t-tests on a large number of dependent variables in the same command, you may get an error message saying that you have specified too many dependent variables. In that case, you should reduce the number of variables you want t-tests on and just use several T-TEST commands.

The non-parametric equivalent to the independent t-test is the Mann-Whitney. To perform a Mann-Whitney test comparing the 24 hour craving scores (CRAV1) of the men versus the women (SEX), you would type:

SPSS-X> NPAR TESTS M-W=CRAV1 BY SEX(1,2).

Here are the results displayed by SPSS when you use this command on the data stored in EXAMPLE.DAT:

```
     CRAV1
  by SEX

   Mean Rank    Cases
     26.50       28    SEX = 1.00
     30.50       28    SEX = 2.00
                 --
                 56    Total
                                  Corrected for Ties
         U          W          Z       2-tailed P
       336.0      742.0     -.9381       .3482
```

You are provided with the U value and the Z score which can be derived from it. This is then used by SPSS to calculate the significance level (2-tailed P) which has to be less than .05 for the result to be statistically significant.

As with the t-test, you can perform the Mann-Whitney test on several variables at once. Thus to test for differences between males and females on all the craving scores, you would type:

SPSS-X> NPAR TESTS M-W=CRAV1 CRAV2 CRAV3 CRAV4 BY SEX(1,2).

The numbers in brackets indicate the values that can be taken by the grouping variable (i.e. SEX). In this case 1=females and the 2=males (see Appendix 4).

8.2 Differences between two groups using MINITAB

To carry out an independent t-test using MINITAB, you use the TWOT command (standing for TWO-sample T-test). To use a t-test to determine whether the 24-hour craving scores (C2) of the males are significantly different from those of the females, type the command:

MTB>   TWOT C2 C10

The first variable (C2) is the dependent variable (the one you want to compare), and the second one (C10) is the independent variable (the one which defines which groups the subjects belong to). The results provided by MINITAB look like this:

```
TWOSAMPLE T FOR C2
C10   N       MEAN     STDEV    SE MEAN
1     28      2.71     1.33     0.25
2     28      3.21     1.75     0.33

95 PCT CI FOR MU 1 - MU 2: (-1.33, 0.33)
TTEST MU 1 = MU 2 (VS NE): T=-1.20 P=0.23 DF=50.4
```

MINITAB only gives you t-values based on separate estimates of the variances for the two groups (i.e. it does not assume that the two groups have roughly the same variance). The critical part of the display is that which states: T=-1.20 P=0.23 DF=50.4. The p value has to be less than .05 for the difference between the groups to be significant. In this case it is not.

MINITAB has a Mann-Whitney but it requires data to be set out in a non-standard manner so I suggest that you use the Kruskal-Wallis test instead. This is normally used where there are more than two groups being compared but is just as applicable when there are only two groups.

To perform a Kruskal-Wallis test comparing the 24-hour craving scores (C2) of the males versus the females (C10), you type:

MTB>   KRUS C2 C10

The results are shown below:

```
LEVEL    NOBS    MEDIAN   AVE. RANK   Z VALUE
1        28      2.500    26.5        -0.92
2        28      3.000    30.5         0.92
OVERALL  56               28.5

H = 0.84    d.f.=1    p=0.359
H = 0.88    d.f.=1    p=0.348 (adj. for ties)
```

The figures to look for in the output are H=.88 d.f.=1 p=0.348 (adj. for ties). The p value has to be less than .05 for the results to be significant.

8.3 Differences between more than two groups using SPSS

SPSS has three commands for performing analysis of variance: **ONEWAY, ANOVA and MANOVA.**

With only one grouping variable
ONEWAY carries out a one-way analysis of variance (with only one grouping variable); ANOVA can be used to carry out a one-way, two-way, three-way or multi-way analysis of variance (with one or more grouping variables); MANOVA carries out a multivariate analysis of variance in which there can be one or more dependent variable and one or more grouping variable.

Suppose that you wished to compare the craving scores after 24 hours' abstinence (CRAV1) in the four treatment conditions (COND). You would type in the command:

```
SPSS-X> ONEWAY CRAV1 BY COND(1,4).
```

To adapt this command to your own needs, you should change: the dependent variable name (CRAV1); the grouping variable name (COND); and the numbers in brackets which indicate what values the grouping variable can take on (between 1 and 4 in this case because there are four conditions). The results displayed using this command are given below:

```
    Variable  CRAV1
 By Variable  COND

                        Analysis of Variance

                        Sum of      Mean         F       F
            Source  D.F.  Squares     Squares    Ratio   Prob.
Between Groups     3    105.3571     35.1190   63.9167  .0000

Within Groups     52     28.5714      .5495

Total             55    133.9286
```

This is a conventional ANOVA table. F prob. gives the significance level of the result. In this case it is .0000 which indicates that the p value is so low that it is off the scale (p values in the ANOVA table are printed to four decimal places).

In other words the difference between the conditions is highly statistically significant. An F Prob. less than .05 indicates a significant difference between the groups being compared. You can specify several dependent variables to be analyzed in the one command, as in:

SPSS-X> ONEWAY CRAV1 CRAV2 CRAV3 CRAV4 BY COND(1,4).

which will perform one-way analyses of variance on CRAV1, CRAV2, CRAV3 and CRAV4.

The equivalent non-parametric test to a one-way independent groups analysis of variance is the Kruskal-Wallis. To perform a Kruskal-Wallis test on the 24 hour craving scores to see whether there was a difference between conditions, you would type the command:

SPSS-X> NPAR TESTS K-W=CRAV1 BY COND(1,4).

All you need to change to adapt this to your own purposes is the name of the dependent variable (CRAV1), the grouping variable (COND), and the numbers in brackets which indicate what values the grouping variable might take (in this example integers between 1 and 4 inclusive). The results of this analysis are shown below. You are provided with a Chi-square corrected for ties and an associated Significance level. The latter has to be less than .05 for the difference between the groups to be statistically significant. In this case it is .0000 which means that the result is highly significant.

```
    CRAV1
by COND

Mean Rank     Cases
    47.50        14    COND =     1
    36.79        14    COND =     2
    13.00        14    COND =     3
    16.71        14    COND =     4
                 --
                 56    Total

                                       Corrected for Ties
   CASES    Chi-Square  Significance   Chi-Square  Significance
      56      42.5687        .0000        44.4843        .0000
```

As with the ONEWAY command, you can perform a Kruskal-Wallis test on several dependent variables in the same command. Thus to test for differences in all the craving scores, you would type:

```
SPSS-X> NPAR TESTS K-W=CRAV1 CRAV2 CRAV3 CRAV4 BY COND(1,4).
```

With two or more grouping variables

If you have two or more grouping variables, you should use the ANOVA command. For example, suppose that you wished to compare the effects of the four conditions and sex on craving after 24 hours' abstinence. To carry out this analysis you would type the command:

```
SPSS-X> ANOVA CRAV1 BY COND(1,4) SEX(1,2).
```

The only parts you would need to change for your own data are the variable names and the numbers inside the brackets. The use of these is the same as in the ONEWAY command.

You can specify as many grouping variables as you are ever likely to need - you just put them one after the other. Do not forget to put the values which each variable can take in brackets after it. It is assumed that your variables are fully crossed in a **factorial design**. In the case of the above example, this means that each of the four conditions is represented for both of the sexes. Thus there are eight groups in all.

Note: It does not matter if your groups do not contain the same numbers of cases because SPSS is quite capable of handling such **unbalanced** designs. You should be aware, however, that if the unevenness of group sizes has resulted from anything other than simple chance fluctuation or if it lead to differences between the variances of the groups, the results of your analysis will be suspect.

The results displayed when using this command are shown below.

```
                   CRAV1
            BY     COND
                   SEX
```

Source of Variation	Sum of Squares	DF	Mean Square	F	Signif of F
Main Effects	108.857	4	27.214	62.630	.000
COND	105.357	3	35.119	80.822	.000
SEX	3.500	1	3.500	8.055	.007
2-way Interactions	4.214	3	1.405	3.233	.030
COND SEX	4.214	3	1.405	3.233	.030
Explained	113.071	7	16.153	37.174	.000
Residual	20.857	48	.435		
Total	133.929	55	2.435		

This is a conventional ANOVA table. The "Signif of F" column give the significance levels (or p values) of the two variables COND and SEX and the two-way interaction between them. All are less than .05 and so all are statistically significant. To find out whether a particular difference is significant, you find the grouping variable or interaction of interest (e.g. COND) and look across to the right hand side of that row to find the corresponding Signif of F.

Planned comparisons
Often when carrying out an analysis of variance, you are not merely interested in whether there is a significant difference between the groups as a whole - rather you think that particular groups might differ from other particular groups. You can ask SPSS to test for these specific differences by using a subcommand within the ONEWAY command.

Suppose, for example, that you wished to examine whether doing something to help craving for cigarettes, was better than doing nothing at all. You would wish to test for a difference between condition 1 (those cases with value 1 in the COND variable), and the other three conditions (acupuncture, tranqillizers, and hypnosis). This could be done by using the command:

SPSS-X> ONEWAY CRAV1 BY COND(1,4) / CONTRAST=-3 1 1 1.

The numbers after the CONTRAST subcommand are weightings to be given to the groups in the variable COND; Group 1 (no treatment) gets a weighting of -3, group 2 (hypnosis), group 3 (acupuncture) and group 4 (tranquillizers) get a weighting of 1 each.

Groups with the same weighting are combined and compared against groups with weightings with opposite sign. This means that group 1 will be compared against groups 2, 3 and 4 combined. You should note that the positive and negative weights must cancel each other out. That is why the first group has a rating of -3.

The relevant portion of the results of this analysis is given below. The contrast (planned comparison) is tested using a t-value (the same as is used in t-tests). You are given the choice of Pooled or Separate Variance estimates. You ought to be able to use the Pooled Variance Estimate because this relies on the assumption that the variances of the groups being compared are broadly similar and this is one of the assumptions underlying the use of analysis of variance anyway. Thus you can use the T value of -11.865. The significance level is given by the T Prob. figure or .000. This is less than .05 so the contrast is significant.

	Grp 1	Grp 2	Grp 3	Grp 4
Contrast 1	-3.0	1.0	1.0	1.0

			Pooled Variance Estimate		
	Value	S. Error	T Value	D.F.	T Prob.
Contrast 1	-8.1429	.6863	-11.865	52.0	.000

			Separate Variance Estimate		
	Value	S. Error	T Value	D.F.	T Prob.
Contrast 1	-8.1429	.9275	-8.779	15.3	.000

You can include zeros in the CONTRAST subcommand. A zero tells SPSS to ignore that group for the purposes of the planned comparison. Suppose that you were interested in whether tranquillizers were more effective in reducing craving after 24 hours than other forms of treatment, you could use the command:

```
SPSS-X> ONEWAY CRAV1 BY COND(1,4) / CONTRAST=0 -1 -1 2.
```

In this example, the first group (no treatment) gets a weighting of 0 and so is discounted. The second and third (hypnosis and acupuncture) both get weightings of -1 and are combined to be compared against group 4 (tranquillizers) which gets a weighting of 2 to balance out the other two groups.

Some misconceptions
Contrary to what is sometimes taught, the overall difference between groups does not have to be significant for you to test for specific differences using planned comparisons. Also, if you use two or more planned comparisons, they do not have to be **orthogonal** (statistically independent of each other). If they are not orthogonal, however, you should mention that they cannot be regarded as independent tests.

Unplanned or post-hoc tests using SPSS
Sometimes, you find a difference between three or more groups using the ONEWAY command, and you want to get some idea where the differences lie. Is it between group 1 and all the others, or between groups 2 and 3 versus the rest, or what? You should NOT carry out a planned comparison in this case because you did not formulate a hypothesis in advance about where the differences would lie. This may seem a subtle distinction because it is in the mind of the experimenter at the time the study was carried out. However it is important statistically.

The ONEWAY command has a facility for carrying out such **unplanned** or **post-hoc** comparisons. Suppose that you had not decided in advance where any differences between conditions in EXAMPLE.DAT would lie. Having observed a statistically significant effect of condition on 24 hour craving scores using the standard ONEWAY procedure, you then want to know which groups were different from which. You would type the command:

SPSS-X> ONEWAY CRAV1 BY COND(1,4) /RANGES=SCHEFFE(.05).

Most of this command is the same as you encountered before for simple one-way analysis of variance. The post-hoc comparison is requested using the RANGES subcommand. In this example, I have chosen Scheffe's multiple comparison test.

The number in brackets indicates the significance level to be used in determining which groups are different from which. In this case I have chosen the conventional level of .05.

The relevant part of the results of this analysis is shown below. The asterisks in the upper part of this output show which groups are statistically different from which other groups in a post-hoc comparison. For example, there is an asterisk in the row corresponding to Group 1 and the column corresponding to Group 2. This indicates that Group 1 differs significantly from Group 2. Group 1 is also shown to differ from Groups 3 and 4. Group 3 differs from Groups 1 and 2 but not Group 4.

```
        Variable  CRAV1
        (Continued)
                             G G G G
                             r r r r
                             p p p p

        Mean       Group     3 4 2 1

        1.5714     Grp 3
        1.8571     Grp 4
        3.4286     Grp 2     * *
        5.0000     Grp 1     * * *
---------------------------------------------------------------------
     Homogeneous Subsets  (Subsets of groups, whose highest and lowest means
                           do not differ by more than the shortest
                           significant range for a subset of that size)

SUBSET  1
Group        Grp 3           Grp 4
Mean         1.5714          1.8571
- - - - - - - - - - - - - -

SUBSET  2
Group        Grp 2
Mean         3.4286
- - - - - - - - -

SUBSET  3
Group        Grp 1
Mean         5.0000
- - - - - - - - -
```

The lower part of the output reveals in another way that Groups 3 and 4 are not statistically separable from each other but both differ from Groups 2 and 1 and each of these two groups differs from all the other groups.

8.4 Differences between more than two groups using MINITAB

MINITAB can perform a one-way analysis of variance whether or not there are the same numbers of cases in each group. However when performing an analysis of variance with two or more grouping variables, it requires each cell to have the same number of cases (i.e. it requires **balanced designs**).

With only one grouping variable
To determine whether there is a difference between the 24 hour craving scores of the four groups (no treatment, hypnosis, etc.) in EXAMPLE.DAT, you would type in the command:

MTB>   ONEWAY C2 C11

This means: perform a one-way analysis of variance on the craving scores in C2, using the conditions (C11) as the grouping variable. The results are displayed below:

```
ANALYSIS OF VARIANCE ON C2
SOURCE      DF        SS         MS          F         p
C11          3    105.357     35.119      63.92     0.000
ERROR       52     28.571      0.549
TOTAL       55    133.929
                                     INDIVIDUAL 95 PCT CI'S FOR MEAN
                                     BASED ON POOLED STDEV
LEVEL        N       MEAN      STDEV   -+---------+---------+---------+-----
  1         14     5.0000     1.1094                               (---*--)
  2         14     3.4286     0.5136                     (---*--)
  3         14     1.5714     0.6462    (--*--)
  4         14     1.8571     0.5345       (--*---)
                                     -+---------+---------+---------+-----
POOLED STDEV =     0.7412             1.2       2.4       3.6       4.8
```

The analysis of variance table includes an F-value (63.92) and its associated p value (significance level). In this case the p value is 0.000 (to three decimal places) which is less than .05 so the difference between the conditions can be regarded as significant.

In addition to the analysis of variance table, MINITAB

provides a graphical representation of the differences between the groups by plotting their means and 95 percent confidence intervals (the range in which there is a 95 percent probability that the true population mean for that group lies). This shows clearly that groups 1 and 2 differ from each other and from groups 3 and 4 but that groups 3 and 4 are indistinguishable from each other (their 95 percent confidence intervals overlap).

To use the Kruskal-Wallis test to assess a difference in 24 hours cravings scores (C2) between the four conditions (C11), you type:

MTB>   KRUS C2 C11

This says: test for differences in C2 between groups specified in C11. The results are shown below:

```
LEVEL      NOBS     MEDIAN  AVE. RANK    Z VALUE
    1        14      5.000      47.5       5.03
    2        14      3.000      36.8       2.19
    3        14      1.500      13.0      -4.11
    4        14      2.000      16.7      -3.12
OVERALL      56                 28.5

H = 42.57   d.f. = 3    p=0.000
H = 44.48   d.f. = 3    p=0.000 (adj. for ties)
```

The figures to look out for are H=44.48 d.f.=3 p=0.000 (adj. for ties). The fact that p<.05 indicates that the difference between the groups is significant.

With two or more grouping variables
If you want to test for differences between two or more grouping variables, you use the ANOVA command; but you must remember that the cell sizes have to be equal.

Suppose, for example, that you wished to examine differences between males and females and between the four conditions in EXAMPLE.DAT using a two-way analysis of variance. As it turns out this would be alright because there are seven subjects in each of the eight cells produced by crossing the four conditions with the two sexes. To perform a two-way analysis of variance with condition (C11) and sex (C10) as the grouping

variables and craving at 24 hours (C2) as the dependent
variable, you type:

MTB>   ANOVA C2=C10 C11 C10*C11

This performs an analysis of variance on the data in C2, using
C10 and C11 as the grouping variables and looking for **main
effects** of C10 and C11 as well as any **interaction** between
them (given by C10*C11).

The results of this are shown below:

```
Factor      Type Levels Values
C10         fixed     2     1     2
C11         fixed     4     1     2     3     4

Analysis of Variance for C2

Source      DF          SS          MS        F       P
C10          1       3.500      3.5000     8.05   0.007
C11          3     105.357     35.1190    80.82   0.000
C10*C11      3       4.214      1.4048     3.23   0.030
Error       48      20.857      0.4345
Total       55     133.929      2.4351
```

The display includes a conventional ANOVA table with F
values and associated significance levels (the p column). To see
whether a particular factor is significant you find the row
corresponding to that factor (e.g. C10 for sex) and look across
to the p value. If this is less than .05 the difference between
the groups in this factor is significant.

8.5 Conclusion

This chapter has covered what are probably the most often used
significance tests in Psychology. You can see that in SPSS it
is relatively easy to enter commands to perform simple
independent t-tests and analyses of variance. In one-way
analyses of variance you can also carry out planned and
unplanned comparisons. MINITAB is more limited. You can
carry out t-tests and one-way and multi-way analyses of
variance. However, the multi-way analyses of variance require
the same numbers of subjects in every group, and there is no
provision for planned or unplanned comparisons. SPSS

provides for Mann-Whitney and Kruskal-Wallis tests to examine differences between groups when the dependent variable cannot be assumed to be normally distributed. The Mann-Whitney substitutes for the independent t-test and the Kruskal-Wallis for the one-way analysis of variance. In MINITAB you only have Kruskal-Wallis (assuming your data are conventionally set out as described in this volume). However, the result is exactly the same as would be found with Mann-Whitney.

All of the tests described in this chapter have been concerned with differences between independent groups of subjects. The next chapter looks at tests used to compare two or more variables each provided by the same subject.

Chapter 9

Differences between repeated measures

This chapter deals with significance tests used to indicate whether differences between two or more variables provided by the same subjects could have come about just by chance or whether they reflect a genuine difference.

Which test to use?

When you are comparing two or more variables provided by the same subjects, you use what are known as **repeated measures, related,** or **within-subject** tests. These terms are used interchangeably.

When there are just **two** measures to be compared from the same case, and the data are normally distributed or the sample size is large, you can use a **related t-test** (also called **paired t-test**). When there are two measures from the same case and the data are not normally distributed you can use a **Wilcoxon**.

When there are **more than two** measures to be compared from the same case and the data are normally distributed or the sample size is large, you can use a **repeated measures ANOVA** (analysis of variance). When there are more than two measures to be compared from the same case and the data are not normally distributed you can use the **Friedman** test.

The Wilcoxon and Friedman are **non-parametric** tests whereas the related t-test and repeated measures ANOVA are **parametric.**

9.1 Related t-test and Wilcoxon using SPSS

The examples in this chapter assume that you have created the data file EXAMPLE.DAT given in Appendix 4 and have begun an SPSS session, read in the data file and recoded the missing values. Chapter 5 gives you the necessary commands.

Suppose that you wished to know whether the craving scores at 24 hours (CRAV1) in EXAMPLE.DAT were significantly different from those at 48 hours (CRAV2). You would type the command:

SPSS-X> T-TEST PAIRS=CRAV1 CRAV2.

The only thing you would need to change for your own data would be the names of the variables involved (CRAV1 and CRAV2). The results are shown below:

```
Paired samples t-test:  CRAV1
                        CRAV2

Variable      Number                 Standard     Standard
            of Cases     Mean       Deviation      Error

CRAV1          56        2.9643       1.560        .209
CRAV2          56        2.6071       1.303        .174


(Difference) Standard    Standard  |    2-Tail    |   t    Degrees of  2-Tail
   Mean     Deviation     Error    | Corr. Prob.  | Value   Freedom    Prob.

   .3571       .841        .112    |  .843  .000  | 3.18      55        .002
```

The main part of the output is the t Value on the right hand side and the associated 2-Tail Prob. which is the significance level of the comparison between the two conditions. This has to be less than .05 for the difference to be statistically significant.

The output also informs you of the correlation between the two variables. In this case it is .843 and is significant at p=.000 (to within three decimal places). This is helpful in that unless the two variables are relatively highly correlated, using a related t-test as opposed to an independent t-test actually loses power; that is, if there is a genuine difference between the conditions in the real world the related t-test is less likely to detect it than an independent t-test.

The command for comparing CRAV1 and CRAV2 using a Wilcoxon would be:

```
SPSS-X> NPAR TESTS WILCOXON=CRAV1 WITH CRAV2.
```

The results are given below:

```
Mean Rank    Cases
    16.08       24   - Ranks (CRAV2 Lt CRAV1)
    15.71        7   + Ranks (CRAV2 Gt CRAV1)
               25     Ties   (CRAV2 Eq CRAV1)
               --
               56     Total

    Z =   -2.7043              2-tailed P =   .0068
```

The W statistic is converted to a Z score (-2.70403) which is then used to calculate a significance level (2-tailed $P = .0068$).

9.2 Related t-test and Wilcoxon using MINITAB

MINITAB does not have any tests directly usable for examining differences between repeated measures. To perform a paired or related t-test, you have to do the following:

1. Use the **LET** command to derive a new variable which is the difference between the two variables you wish to compare.

2. Use a **one sample t-test** to assess whether that variable is significantly different from 0.

This is a little cumbersome but it is arithmetically identical to performing a related t-test. Thus, if you wished to know whether the craving scores at 24 hours in EXAMPLE.DAT were different from those at 48 hours, you could type in the commands:

```
MTB>    LET C25=C2-C4
MTB>    TTEST C25
```

The results are shown below:

```
TEST OF MU = 0.000 VS MU N.E. 0.000

            N      MEAN    STDEV   SE MEAN        T    P VALUE
C25        56     0.357    0.841     0.112     3.18     0.0024
```

This output supplies a T value and associated P VALUE (significance level). In this example T=3.18 which is significant at .0024 (to four decimal places). This is less than .05 so the difference between conditions is significant.

If the differences between the variables you are comparing (e.g. those held in C25) cannot be assumed to be normally distributed, you can use a one sample Wilcoxon instead of the one sample t-test. Thus, you could use the commands:

MTB>   LET C25=C2-C4
MTB>   WTEST C25

The results are shown below:

```
TEST OF MEDIAN = 0.000000000 VERSUS MEDIAN N.E. 0.000000000

          N FOR    WILCOXON            ESTIMATED
          N   TEST STATISTIC  P-VALUE     MEDIAN
C25      56    31      386.0    0.007     0.5000
```

The W value is 386.0 and the associated significance level (P-VALUE) is .007. The N FOR TEST of 31 means that only 31 of the 56 subjects had different values (one way or the other) for the two variables (C2 and C4) being compared.

9.3 Repeated measures ANOVA and Friedman using SPSS

Repeated measures analysis of variance is available in SPSS, but you have to know when you can and cannot use it. Moreover, you have to know when you can use **averaged tests of significance** (the same as a conventional **univariate F-ratio** as taught in undergraduate courses), and when you should use one of the **multivariate statistics** which are provided.

In general, if the **residuals** in your data (what is left once you have taken out any specific effects due to differences between conditions) are normally distributed, you can use a repeated measures analysis of variance. If the variables you are comparing all correlate with each other to roughly the same degree you can use the averaged tests of significance, otherwise you should use the multivariate statistics.

The examples which follow will make this somewhat clearer. They assume that you have created the data file EXAMPLE.DAT and then begun an SPSS session, read in the data file and recoded the missing values. Chapter 5 gives you the necessary commands if you are unsure.

I will deal first of all with the situation when there is only one within-subject factor, and then consider multi-way designs.

Single factor designs
Suppose that you wished to know whether there was a difference between the craving scores in EXAMPLE.DAT taken at four different times after smoking cessation (24 hours, 48 hours, 72 hours and 96 hours). You would use the command:

```
SPSS-X>  MANOVA CRAV1 CRAV2 CRAV3 CRAV4 / WSFACTORS
CONT>    =TIME(4).
```

This command says:

- Perform a multivariate analysis of variance (what SPSS uses to carry out any repeated measures analysis of variance) on the variables CRAV1, CRAV2, CRAV3 and CRAV4.

- Call the within-subject factor represented by these four variables "TIME". (You could have used any name you wished.) The 4 in brackets tells SPSS that there are four different variables that you want to compare (CRAV1, CRAV2 etc.).

To carry out a similar analysis on your own data all you would need to change are the names of the variables you want to compare (CRAV1, CRAV2 etc.), the name you give to the within-subject factor (TIME), and the number of **levels** of that factor (4).

Note: The number of levels of the factor must be the same as the number of variables you are comparing with each other.

The main parts of the output are given below:

```
Tests of Between-Subjects Effects.

Tests of Significance for T1 using UNIQUE sums of squares
Source of Variation          SS        DF        MS         F  Sig of F

WITHIN CELLS              206.48       55      3.75
CONSTANT                 1254.02        1   1254.02    334.03     .000

- - - - - - - - - -

Tests involving 'TIME' Within-Subject Effect.


Mauchly sphericity test, W =         .45568
Chi-square approx.        =     42.22393 with 5 D. F.
Significance =                       .000

Greenhouse-Geisser Epsilon =         .64382
Huynh-Feldt Epsilon =                .66682
Lower-bound Epsilon =                .33333


EFFECT .. TIME
Multivariate Tests of Significance (S = 1, M = 1/2, N = 25 1/2)

Test Name          Value  Approx. F Hypoth. DF   Error DF  Sig. of F

Pillais           .43386  13.53884       3.00      53.00      .000
Hotellings        .76635  13.53884       3.00      53.00      .000
Wilks             .56614  13.53884       3.00      53.00      .000
Roys              .43386

- - - - - - - - - - -
Tests involving 'TIME' Within-Subject Effect.

AVERAGED Tests of Significance for CRAV using UNIQUE sums of squares
Source of Variation          SS        DF        MS         F  Sig of F

WITHIN CELLS              122.20      165       .74
TIME                       57.30        3     19.10     25.79     .000

- - - - - - - - - -
```

The first section of output relating to Between-Subjects Effects can be ignored.

If result of the Mauchly sphericity test is **significant**, the correlations between the variables we are using are not all roughly the same and we should use the **multivariate statistics**. There are three to choose from: **Pillais, Hotellings** and **Wilks**. They all give roughly the same significance values (**Sig. of F.**). I suggest you use Hotellings. In this example the significance level is .000 to three decimal places.

If Mauchly' sphericity test is not significant, you can use the **AVERAGED tests of significance**. These are shown in a standard analysis of variance table with sums of squares, mean squares and degrees of freedom. The F value in this example is 25.79 and the significance level (Sig of F) is .000 to three decimal places.

If the residuals cannot be assumed to be normally distributed, then you can use the Friedman test. For the example just used, this is done by typing the command:

```
SPSS-X> NPAR TESTS FRIEDMAN=CRAV1 CRAV2 CRAV3 CRAV4.
```

The only thing you would need to change to adapt the command to your own needs would be the list of variables you wished to compare (CRAV1, CRAV2 etc.).

The results are shown below:

```
Mean Rank   Variable

    3.13    CRAV1
    2.71    CRAV2
    2.29    CRAV3
    1.86    CRAV4

    Cases        Chi-Square      D.F.    Significance
      56           30.3482         3         .0000
```

The Friedman test yields a Chi-square value and associated significance level. The latter has to be less than .05 for the difference between the conditions to be statistically significant.

Multi-factorial designs
If there are two or more repeated measures factors, you can

still use the MANOVA command. Suppose, for example, that you wanted to test whether there were any differences between the craving scores at the four different times (24 hours etc.) and also whether these craving scores were higher or lower than difficulty not smoking scores taken at the same time. Suppose in addition, that you wanted to know whether changes in the craving scores over time differed from changes in the difficulty not smoking scores. You would type in a command like this:

```
SPSS-X> MANOVA CRAV1 CRAV2 CRAV3 CRAV4 DIFF1 DIFF2
CONT>    DIFF3 DIFF4 / WSFAC = SCORETYP(2) TIME(4).
```

This tells SPSS to perform a repeated measures analysis of variance on the variables CRAV1, CRAV2, CRAV3, ..., DIFF3 and DIFF4. These variables are to be considered as two within-subject factors (TIME and SCORETYP). The factor TIME has four levels (there are four different time points), and the factor SCORETYP has two levels (there are two different score types, craving and difficulty not smoking).

You might be asking yourself how SPSS knows which variables contribute to the TIME factor and which ones contribute to the SCORETYP factor. The answer is **by the order in which you list the variables in the command**. The first set of variables always matches up to the different levels of the LAST within-subject factor specified. Thus CRAV1, CRAV2, CRAV3 and CRAV4 match up to the four levels of TIME. Then these taken together form the first level of the second factor mentioned (SCORETYP). Thus CRAV1, CRAV2, CRAV3 and CRAV4 represent the first level of score type, and DIFF1, DIFF2, DIFF3 and DIFF4 represent the second level of score type.

You can probably see this more clearly if I give another example with the variables and the within-subject factors in a different order:

```
SPSS-X> MANOVA CRAV1 DIFF1 CRAV2 DIFF2 CRAV3 DIFF3
CONT>    CRAV4 DIFF4 / WSFAC = TIME(4) SCORETYP(2).
```

In this case, CRAV1 and DIFF1 represent the first and second levels of the last within-subject factor mentioned (SCORETYP), while CRAV1 and DIFF1 combined represent the first level of the TIME factor. The way that this is sometimes expressed is by saying that the factor which cycles through the variable list most slowly is mentioned first in the WSFAC list.

The numbers in brackets multiplied together must equal the number of variables in the variable list. In this example, the levels of SCORETYP are 2 and the levels of TIME are 4, and 4 times 2 is 8; there are eight variables so all is well.

Shown below are the main parts of the results of this last command. Notice that SPSS uses the name you gave to the within-subject factors when reporting the results. You could have given any names you wished (up to eight characters long).

```
Tests involving 'TIME' Within-Subject Effect.

Mauchly sphericity test, W =        .47963
Chi-square approx. =         39.47136 with 5 D. F.
Significance =               .000

Greenhouse-Geisser Epsilon =      .67642
Huynh-Feldt Epsilon =             .70252
Lower-bound Epsilon =             .33333

EFFECT .. TIME
Multivariate Tests of Significance (S = 1, M = 1/2, N = 25 1/2)

Test Name       Value  Approx. F Hypoth. DF   Error DF  Sig. of F

Pillais         .49478  17.30144      3.00       53.00      .000
Hotellings      .97933  17.30144      3.00       53.00      .000
Wilks           .50522  17.30144      3.00       53.00      .000
Roys            .49478

- - - - - - - - - -
Tests involving 'TIME' Within-Subject Effect.

AVERAGED Tests of Significance for MEAS.1 using UNIQUE sums of squares
Source of Variation          SS       DF        MS        F  Sig of F

WITHIN CELLS              89.22      165       .54
TIME                      46.03        3     15.34    28.37      .000

Tests involving 'SCORETYP' Within-Subject Effect.

Tests of Significance for T5 using UNIQUE sums of squares
Source of Variation          SS       DF        MS        F  Sig of F

WITHIN CELLS             109.24       55      1.99
SCORETYP                  15.01        1     15.01     7.56      .008
```

```
Tests involving 'TIME BY SCORETYP' Within-Subject Effect.

Mauchly sphericity test, W =        .49953
Chi-square approx. =           37.28744 with 5 D. F.
Significance =                      .000

Greenhouse-Geisser Epsilon =        .66909
Huynh-Feldt Epsilon =               .69448
Lower-bound Epsilon =               .33333

EFFECT .. TIME BY SCORETYP
Multivariate Tests of Significance (S = 1, M = 1/2, N = 25 1/2)

Test Name        Value  Approx. F Hypoth. DF   Error DF  Sig. of F

Pillais          .30077  7.59908       3.00      53.00      .000
Hotellings       .43014  7.59908       3.00      53.00      .000
Wilks            .69923  7.59908       3.00      53.00      .000
Roys             .30077

Tests involving 'TIME BY SCORETYP' Within-Subject Effect.

AVERAGED Tests of Significance for MEAS.1 using UNIQUE sums of squares
Source of Variation           SS      DF       MS         F   Sig of F

WITHIN CELLS                78.08     165      .47
TIME BY SCORETYP            15.67       3     5.22     11.04      .000

- - - - - - - - - -
```

The results for TIME are given first, then the results for SCORETYP and then the results for the interaction between TIME and SCORETYP. In each case you are given diagnostic statistics including Mauchly's sphericity test. This is followed by the multivariate tests of significance and the averaged tests of significance. For further explanation of these, see earlier in the chapter. You may have noticed, however, that the set of diagnostic statistics including Mauchly's sphericity test is not given for the SCORETYP factor. This is because there are only two levels of this factor (two possible score types, craving and difficulty not smoking). In that case the issue of whether correlations between the variables that make up the factor are similar does not arise because there is only one possible correlation. Moreover, only univariate F ratios can be calculated.

SPSS allows you to carry out repeated measures analyses of variance with as many within-subject factors as you are likely to need. You just have to make sure that the variable list matches the within-subject factors (WSFAC) list in terms of the order in which the variables are specified and the number of variables and factors used.

Planned comparisons

The MANOVA command allows you to perform planned comparisons between particular repeated measures conditions. Unfortunately, it does not do quite what you would expect, and the way that the results are displayed is somewhat obscure. If you are a little shaky about repeated measures analysis of variance generally, then you had probably better skip this section for the time being.

Suppose that in EXAMPLE.DAT you had reason to believe that the 24 hour craving scores would be significantly higher than all the others (i.e. that there would be a sharp reduction in craving after 24 hours and little change thereafter). You could type in the following command:

```
SPSS-X> MANOVA CRAV1 CRAV2 CRAV3 CRAV4 / WSFACTORS
CONT>   =TIME(4) /CONTRAST(TIME) = SPECIAL(1 1 1 1 -3 1 1 1
CONT>   0 -2 1 1 0 0 -1 1) / PRINT = SIGNIF(UNIV).
```

Everything in this command up to the CONTRAST statement is familiar. The CONTRAST statement says: carry out a SPECIAL contrast (as opposed to one of the ready-made ones which SPSS provides), made up as specified by the **weights** in the brackets. These should be read as follows:

```
(      1       1       1       1
      -3       1       1       1
       0      -2       1       1
       0       0      -1       1            )
```

Each line after the first refers to a particular contrast (planned comparison), so in fact you have requested three contrasts. You may only be interested in one of these but you have to specify all of them nonetheless! The number of contrasts requested must always be one less than the levels of the factor concerned.

The first line always just has 1s in it. The number of weights in each row must correspond to the number of levels of the factor. TIME has four levels so there are four 1s. The second line is the contrast we are interested in. I specified a weight of -3 for the first variable (which is CRAV1 in the variable list), and 1 each for the other three variables. SPSS combines variables with the same number (1 in this case) and compares them with variables with the opposite sign (-3). **The positive numbers must cancel out the negative numbers.** Thus the three 1s counterbalance the -3.

The remaining lines are just there because SPSS requires them - but they cannot be just any numbers. The remaining contrasts must be **orthogonal** to each other and to the one you are interested in; if they are not, then SPSS automatically changes all the contrasts so that they are, and the result is that you do not get the result you want. One way to ensure that the remaining contrasts are orthogonal is only to contrast variables which have been **combined** or **ignored** in previous contrasts. Thus, in the third line I have set the first variable to 0 telling SPSS that it is not to be used in this contrast and then compared the second variable with the third and fourth. In the fourth line, I have set the first and second variables to 0 and just compared the third and fourth variable.

Note: You may of course be interested in one or more of the contrasts that you have used.

The PRINT command tells SPSS to print the results of the contrasts. The relevant part of the resulting output is shown below:

```
Univariate F-tests with (1,55) D. F.

Variable   Hypoth. SS   Error SS Hypoth. MS   Error MS        F  Sig. of F

T2          26.72024   38.11310   26.72024    .69297   38.55927      .000
T3          16.29762   38.36905   16.29762    .69762   23.36177      .000
T4          14.28571   45.71429   14.28571    .83117   17.18750      .000
```

The results of the planned comparison are presented at the end of the standard MANOVA output. You should focus on the F-ratio corresponding to T2. T3 gives the results of the second contrast (0 -2 1 1), and T4 gives the results of the third contrast (0 0 -1 1). Since both of these were used just to satisfy SPSS's rather idiosyncratic requirements they will probably not be of interest to you. In this example, the F value for T2 is 38.55927 which has a corresponding significance level of .000 (to three decimal places). The latter is less than .05 so the contrast is significant. This means that craving at 24 hours was significantly different from the average of the other three craving scores. This does not imply that there is then no difference between these other three craving ratings.

9.4 Repeated measures ANOVA using MINITAB

It is possible to perform a repeated measures analysis of variance using MINITAB but it requires the data to be in a non-standard format and to avoid confusion I have not covered it in this book. There is also the problem that it only performs a univariate repeated measures analysis of variance for which the assumptions are very often violated (see discussion of Mauchly's sphericity test in preceding sections).

9.5 Conclusion

You should now be able to carry out repeated measures analyses on your data. When using analysis of variance, it is more complicated than when you have an independent groups design. SPSS also allows you to perform a non-parametric repeated measures analysis of variance using the Friedman test.

Chapter 10

Differences between groups and between repeated measures

Often in Psychology one uses designs which involve one or more repeated measures factors as well as one or more independent groups factors. The way to handle such designs is with a **mixed** ANOVA. SPSS uses the MANOVA command for this. MINITAB has no such facility but in simple designs where there are only two levels of the repeated measures factors, it is relatively easy to construct arithmetically equivalent analyses of variance.

10.1 Analyzing mixed designs using SPSS

This chapter assumes that you have created a data file EXAMPLE.DAT as described in Appendix 4, and then begun an SPSS session, read in the data file and recoded the missing values. Chapter 5 gives the commands for doing this in case you are unsure.

Suppose that you wished to examine the effects of the various conditions (COND) on craving scores measured at 24 hours, 48 hours, 72 hours and 96 hours, and you also wanted to know whether craving varied across the different time points and whether craving in the different treatment conditions followed different time courses.

The effect of COND would be the same as was found using the ONEWAY command in Chapter 8. The effect of time when the measures were taken would be broadly (but not precisely) the same as was found for the TIME factor using the MANOVA command in Chapter 9. What one also wants, however, is an assessment of the **interaction** between TIME and COND. This will tell you whether the conditions have different effects in reducing craving at different times. Tranquillizers might be most effective early on while hypnosis may be more effective later (pure speculation). To perform the two-way analysis of variance, you would type the command:

```
SPSS-X> MANOVA CRAV1 CRAV2 CRAV3 CRAV4 BY COND (1,4)
CONT>    / WSFAC = TIME(4).
```

You can see that this is just like the repeated measures analysis of variance as described in Chapter 9 but with a BY COND(1,4) added. This gets SPSS to perform the repeated measures analysis and the between groups analysis together. The relevant parts of the output are shown below.

```
Tests of Between-Subjects Effects.

Tests of Significance for T1 using UNIQUE sums of squares
Source of Variation           SS         DF         MS          F   Sig of F

WITHIN CELLS                68.14        52       1.31
CONSTANT                  1254.02         1    1254.02     956.94       .000
COND                       138.34         3      46.11      35.19       .000
- - - - - - - - - -

Tests involving 'TIME' Within-Subject Effect.

Mauchly sphericity test, W =           .88322
Chi-square approx. =              6.29852 with 5 D. F.
Significance =                     .278

Greenhouse-Geisser Epsilon =       .93373
Huynh-Feldt Epsilon =             1.00000
Lower-bound Epsilon =              .33333

EFFECT .. COND BY TIME
Multivariate Tests of Significance (S = 3, M = -1/2, N = 24 )

Test Name       Value   Approx. F Hypoth. DF    Error DF  Sig. of F
Pillais       1.00940    8.78939       9.00      156.00       .000
Hotellings    3.79866   20.54089       9.00      146.00       .000
Wilks          .17128   14.41346       9.00      121.84       .000
Roys           .77817
- - - - - - - - - -

EFFECT .. TIME
Multivariate Tests of Significance (S = 1, M = 1/2, N = 24 )

Test Name       Value   Approx. F Hypoth. DF    Error DF  Sig. of F
Pillais        .76895   55.46658       3.00       50.00       .000
Hotellings    3.32799   55.46658       3.00       50.00       .000
Wilks          .23105   55.46658       3.00       50.00       .000
Roys           .76895
- - - - - - - - - -
Tests involving 'TIME' Within-Subject Effect.

AVERAGED Tests of Significance for CRAV using UNIQUE sums of squares
Source of Variation           SS         DF         MS          F  Sig of F

WITHIN CELLS                54.43       156        .35
TIME                        57.30         3      19.10      54.75       .000
COND BY TIME                67.77         9       7.53      21.58       .000
```

The output begins with an analysis of between-subject effects. This includes an analysis of whether there was an overall difference between the conditions on the four craving scores combined. This is followed by diagnostic statistics concerning the within-subject variable (TIME). In this case the sphericity test is not significant and we would be entitled to use the averaged tests of significance. Then SPSS provides the multivariate test of the COND by TIME interaction followed by the multivariate test of the TIME factor. Given that the sphericity test was not significant, we do not need to use these results and can move directly to the AVERAGED tests of significance which includes the TIME factor and the TIME by COND interaction in a single table. The fact that the TIME by COND interaction is significant indicates that the time course of craving did differ according to which treatment condition the subjects were in.

See Chapter 9 for a more detailed interpretation of the repeated measures output.

The addition of more factors to either the repeated measures or the between-subjects list follows a predictable pattern. Suppose that you wanted to examine the effects of condition (COND) and sex (SEX), both of which are between-subjects factors, on craving at different times versus difficulty not smoking at different times (two within-subject factors). The command would go like this:

```
SPSS-X> MANOVA CRAV1 CRAV2 CRAV3 CRAV4 DIFF1 DIFF2
CONT>   DIFF3 DIFF4 BY COND(1,4) SEX(1,2) / WSFAC =
CONT>   SCORETYP(2) TIME (4).
```

The construction of this command should be clear from reading Chapters 8 and 9.

10.2 Simple mixed designs using MINITAB

Although MINITAB does not have facilities for repeated measures analysis of variance and hence cannot handle mixed designs, it is possible to fudge it as long as the within-subject factors have only **two levels**. Suppose, for example, that you wished to examine the effect of condition on craving scores versus difficulty not smoking scores. You could do it like this:

```
MTB>    LET C25=C2+C4+C6+C8
MTB>    LET C26=C3+C5+C7+C9
MTB>    LET C27=C25+C26
MTB>    LET C28=C25-C26
MTB>    ONEWAY C27 C11
MTB>    ONEWAY C28 C11
```

What this series of commands does is to calculate total scores for craving and for difficulty not smoking (C25 and C26). It then calculates a total score for the two combined (C27). Then it calculates a score for the difference between the craving and difficulty not smoking scores (C28). The ONEWAY carried out on C27 tests for a difference between the conditions on the scores as a whole. Finally the ONEWAY on C28 tests the interaction between condition and type of score, i.e. whether the various conditions have different effects on craving versus difficulty not smoking.

The results of these analyses are shown below:

```
ANALYSIS OF VARIANCE ON C27
SOURCE     DF        SS        MS        F         p
C11         3     1793.5     597.8     34.24    0.000
ERROR      52      907.9      17.5
TOTAL      55     2701.4
                                      INDIVIDUAL 95 PCT CI'S FOR MEAN
                                      BASED ON POOLED STDEV
LEVEL       N      MEAN      STDEV    --------+---------+---------+--------
    1       14    29.929     5.030                              (---*---)
    2       14    19.286     2.268                (---*---)
    3       14    16.643     5.257        (---*--)
    4       14    15.714     3.429    (---*---)
                                      --------+---------+---------+--------
POOLED STDEV =     4.178                 18.0      24.0      30.0


ANALYSIS OF VARIANCE ON C28
SOURCE     DF        SS        MS        F         p
C11         3      144.9      48.3      3.45     0.023
ERROR      52      729.0      14.0
TOTAL      55      873.9
                                      INDIVIDUAL 95 PCT CI'S FOR MEAN
                                      BASED ON POOLED STDEV
LEVEL       N      MEAN      STDEV    ---+---------+---------+---------+---
    1       14    -1.214     4.191             (-------*-------)
    2       14     0.857     2.931                    (-------*-------)
    3       14    -3.643     3.915    (-------*------)
    4       14    -1.857     3.820          (-------*------)
                                      ---+---------+---------+---------+---
POOLED STDEV =     3.744              -5.0      -2.5       0.0       2.5
```

The analysis of variance on C27 shows that there was a

significant difference between the conditions in the craving and difficulty not smoking scores combined. The analysis of variance on C28 indicates that there was a significant difference between the effect of the different treatment conditions on the craving and difficulty not smoking scores (p=.023). The results are arithmetically the same as would have resulted from a "proper" mixed analysis of variance.

10.3 Conclusion

This chapter concludes our examination of the use of statistical tests to assess the significance of differences between groups and/or experimental conditions. There is a growing belief among psychologists that these traditional statistical tests may not be the best way of treating one's data. For example, many believe that it makes more sense to cite 95 percent confidence intervals. A few also argue that we should adopt a "Baysian" approach in which we continually update our confidence in the experimental propositions in the light of new evidence. However, it is likely that traditional significance testing will remain the main form of analysis for the foreseeable future.

Chapter 11

Multiple Regression

11.1 About multiple regression

If you wish to examine the extent to which each of a set of variables **independently** predicts a dependent variable you can perform a multiple regression. The regression we will consider here involves examining **linear** relationships between the predictor and dependent variables. The two most commonly used forms are **stepwise** and **forced entry**.

Stepwise multiple regression
In stepwise multiple regression, a list of designated predictor variables is specified. These are entered one at a time into a regression equation, starting with the best predictor until there are no new variables which significantly add to the collective predictive power of those already entered. If adding a new variable into the equation causes one which was previously entered no longer to provide an adequate independent prediction of the dependent variable, it is removed from the equation in that step.

At the end of the process some of the designated variables will have been included in the list of significant predictors and some will probably have been left out. For each one which is included, its predictive power, taking into account all the others which have been included, is indicated.

Forced entry multiple regression
In forced entry multiple regression, all the designated predictor variables are entered together and the predictive power of each one taking into account ALL the others is provided.

Non-linearity and interactions
If the relationship between any of the predictor variables and

the dependent variable is not linear, the whole procedure may not be appropriate. This problem can sometimes be alleviated by transforming one of the variables by taking logs or square roots.

Multiple regression as discussed here does not take into account interactions among the predictor variables. It may be that they have effects together which are not merely additive.

11.2 Multiple regression using SPSS

This chapter assumes that you have created the data file EXAMPLE.DAT, begun an SPSS session, read in the data file and recoded the missing values. Chapter 5 indicates how to do this if you are unsure.

Suppose that you wished to know to what extent scores on the smoking motivation questionnaire predicted craving at 24 hours in EXAMPLE.DAT. You could calculate simple Pearson correlations (see Chapter 7) between each of the smoking motivation subscale scores (PSY to ADD) and CRAV1. However some of these subscale scores are correlated with each other so any association with craving might be indirect (just an artifact of their association with another variable which happens to correlate with craving).

Forced entry multiple regression

To carry out a forced entry multiple regression with smoking motivation scores as predictors, and craving at 24 hours as the dependent (predicted) variable, you type the command:

```
SPSS-X> REGRESS VAR=PSY HAND INDUL SED STIM AUTO
CONT>   ADD CRAV1 /DEP=CRAV1 / METHOD=ENTER.
```

The parts that you will need to change for your own data are:

- The list of variables after the VAR=. This should include all the predictor variables that you want included plus the dependent variable (the one to be predicted);

- The variable inserted after the DEP=. This specifies which of the preceding variables is to be the dependent variable. Only one variable is allowed here.

The main parts of the output are shown below. There are several features to look for. First of all there is the statement of Multiple R, Multiple R Square, and adjusted Multiple R Square. The multiple R is the correlation between the combined predictor variables and the dependent variable. The adjusted Multiple R Square indicates the proportion of variance in the dependent variable which is accounted for or explained by the combined predictor variables. In this case 41.8 percent of the variance in CRAV1 is explained by the combined forces of the smoking motivation scores.

```
Equation Number 1     Dependent Variable..   CRAV1

Multiple R           .70150
R Square             .49211
Adjusted R Square    .41804
Standard Error      1.19043

Analysis of Variance
                    DF      Sum of Squares      Mean Square
Regression           7            65.90696          9.41528
Residual            48            68.02162          1.41712

F =       6.64397      Signif F =   .0000


------------------ Variables in the Equation ------------------

Variable              B         SE B        Beta         T    Sig T

ADD              .34988       .06898      .53817     5.073    .0000
HAND            -.15488       .05815     -.29932    -2.663    .0105
AUTO            -.08817       .08847     -.10920     -.997    .3239
INDUL            .01842       .08301      .02349      .222    .8253
STIM       -3.75025E-03       .06562  -6.335E-03     -.057    .9547
PSY             -.18098       .10180     -.19647    -1.778    .0818
SED              .05306       .07893      .07553      .672    .5046
(Constant)      2.65564       .79286                 3.349    .0016
```

The analysis of variance simply provides an indication of whether the combination of the predictor variables does better than chance in predicting the dependent variable. The F of 6.64397 with significance level .0000 indicates a statistically significant level of prediction.

Finally comes a table of regression coefficients (B) and standardized regression coefficients (Beta) for each of the predictor variables, together with t-values (T) used to calculate whether they make a significant **independent** contribution to predicting craving. The rightmost column in this table is in many ways the most important. It shows the significance level of the contribution made by each variable taking account of all the other predictor variables. When reporting the results, you would normally indicate the B and Beta, the t-value and significance level for those dependent variables that make a significant contribution.

In this example, smoking to alleviate craving (ADD) and smoking for something to do with one's hands (HAND) are the only variables which make independent contributions to predicting craving at 24 hours (CRAV1). It is worth noting, however, that the association between ADD and CRAV1 is positive whereas the association between HAND and CRAV1 is negative (the T has a minus sign in front of it). Thus in this fictitious data set smokers who reported that the manipulation of cigarettes was important to them craved less.

Stepwise multiple regression

To carry out a stepwise multiple regression using SPSS, the command is very similar. You would type:

```
SPSS-X> REGRESS VAR=PSY HAND INDUL SED STIM AUTO
CONT>   ADD CRAV1 / DEP=CRAV1 / METHOD=STEP.
```

Notice that the only difference from the previous example is the use of STEP rather than ENTER. The results are perhaps a little more complicated. They are shown below:

```
Variable(s) Entered on Step Number
   1..    ADD

Multiple R            .56172
R Square              .31553
Adjusted R Square     .30285
Standard Error       1.30292

Analysis of Variance
                    DF      Sum of Squares      Mean Square
Regression           1            42.25815         42.25815
Residual            54            91.67042          1.69760

F =     24.89287      Signif F =  .0000
```

```
Equation Number 1    Dependent Variable..   CRAV1

----------------- Variables in the Equation ------------------

Variable            B        SE B      Beta          T  Sig T
ADD            .36519      .07320    .56172      4.989  .0000
(Constant)    1.73828      .30116                5.772  .0000


------------ Variables not in the Equation -------------

Variable     Beta In  Partial  Min Toler         T  Sig T
PSY          -.28618  -.34163     .97541    -2.646  .0107
HAND         -.35984  -.43482     .99944    -3.515  .0009
INDUL      6.4903E-03   .00782     .99261      .057  .9548
SED          -.01761  -.02118     .99031     -.154  .8780
STIM         -.06519  -.07823     .98573     -.571  .5702
AUTO         -.13622  -.16449     .99804    -1.214  .2301

Variable(s) Entered on Step Number
   2..    HAND

Multiple R            .66704
R Square              .44494
Adjusted R Square     .42400
Standard Error       1.18432

Analysis of Variance
                DF    Sum of Squares     Mean Square
Regression       2          59.59049        29.79525
Residual        53          74.33808         1.40261

F =      21.24279        Signif F =   .0000

Equation Number 1    Dependent Variable..   CRAV1

----------------- Variables in the Equation ------------------

Variable            B        SE B      Beta          T  Sig T
ADD            .37073      .06655    .57024      5.571  .0000
HAND         -.18620      .05297   -.35984     -3.515  .0009
(Constant)    2.40462      .33297                7.222  .0000


------------ Variables not in the Equation -------------

Variable     Beta In  Partial  Min Toler         T  Sig T
PSY          -.19315  -.24387     .88490    -1.813  .0756
INDUL         .05861   .07760     .97285      .561  .5770
SED           .04596   .06047     .96099      .437  .6640
STIM      -7.313E-03  -.00962     .96042     -.069  .9450
AUTO         -.08326  -.11034     .97485     -.801  .4270


End Block Number   1    PIN =      .050 Limits reached.
```

As the name "stepwise" indicates, the process occurs in stages.
The events proceed like this:

Step 1
SPSS looks for any variables in the list of designated predictors
which correlate significantly (using Pearson's R) with the
dependent variable.

If it does not find any, then it stops and reports that there are no significant predictors. SPSS does this by telling you that no variables have been entered in the regression equation. (The regression equation is the equation in which values of predictor variables are used to derive values of the dependent variable.) If there is at least one variable which meets the criterion, then the one with the highest correlation with the dependent variable is entered into the regression equation and a report is produced of the R between this variable and the dependent variable, the R Square, and the significance level. A list is also produced of all those variables left out of the regression equation at this stage. The process now goes to step 2.

In this example the variable ADD is entered into the equation in step 1.

Step 2
SPSS looks for any variables in the list of designated predictor variables not currently in the equation which correlate significantly with the dependent variable **having already taken into consideration the contribution made by the variable or variables already in the regression equation.**

If there are none, then the process stops.

If there is at least one variable not currently in the equation which correlates significantly with the dependent variable after the contributions made by those in the equation are taken into account, then the best of these is entered into the regression equation. A new multiple R is displayed as is a new list of variables which are currently in the equation and ones which are not in the equation.

If none of the variables left out of the regression equation after step 1 predicts the dependent variable significantly taking account of the variable in the equation (ADD), the process stops. In this example, there was a second variable (HAND) which made an independent contribution to predicting craving. Therefore at step two both HAND and ADD were included in the list of variables in the equation. The list of variables not in the equation after step 2 contained none with significance levels of less than .05 so the process halted.

Unless you specify otherwise, SPSS uses the .05 level of significance as the **criterion for entering** a new variable into the regression equation in a given step. The **criterion to remove** an existing variable from the regression equation because it no longer contributes significantly to the prediction of the dependent variable is normally set at p<.1 by SPSS.

To make the required significance level to enter a variable .01, and to remove a variable .05, you add /CRITERIA=PIN(.01) POUT(.05) as in:

```
SPSS-X> REGRESS VAR=CRAV1 PSY TO ADD / CRITERIA=
CONT>   PIN(.01) POUT(.05) /DEP=CRAV1 /METHOD=STEP.
```

The CRITERIA command must come after the VAR command and before the DEP command. The PIN(.01) means set the probability (significance level) to enter a variable in the equation at .01 or less; the POUT(.05) means set the probability to keep the variable in the equation at .05 or less.

Note: The criterion to remove a variable (POUT) should be less stringent than the criterion to enter a variable (PIN) to avoid the same variable being alternately entered and removed in successive steps ad infinitum.

11.3 Multiple regression using MINITAB

Forced entry multiple regression
If you wished to determine the individual contributions made by scores on the smoking motivation questionnaires to ratings of craving after 24 hours of abstinence in EXAMPLE.DAT, you would carry out a forced entry multiple regression as follows:

```
MTB>    REGRESS C2 7 C14-C20
```

This tells MINITAB to perform a forced entry multiple regression with C2 (craving after 24 hours) as the dependent variable (the variable to be predicted) with 7 designated predictor variables, namely C14 to C20

The results of this are shown below:

```
The regression equation is
C2 = 2.66 - 0.181 C14 - 0.155 C15 + 0.0184 C16 + 0.0531 C17 - 0.0038 C18
          - 0.0882 C19 + 0.350 C20

Predictor        Coef       Stdev     t-ratio        p
Constant        2.6556     0.7929       3.35      0.002
C14            -0.1810     0.1018      -1.78      0.082
C15            -0.15488    0.05815     -2.66      0.011
C16             0.01842    0.08301      0.22      0.825
C17             0.05306    0.07893      0.67      0.505
C18            -0.00375    0.06562     -0.06      0.955
C19            -0.08817    0.08847     -1.00      0.324
C20             0.34988    0.06898      5.07      0.000

s = 1.190        R-sq = 49.2%      R-sq(adj) = 41.8%

Analysis of Variance

SOURCE          DF         SS          MS         F         p
Regression       7      65.907       9.415      6.64     0.000
Error           48      68.022       1.417
Total           55     133.929

SOURCE          DF       SEQ SS
C14              1       18.061
C15              1        8.268
C16              1        0.081
C17              1        1.320
C18              1        0.073
C19              1        1.639
C20              1       36.464

Unusual Observations
Obs.      C14         C2      Fit  Stdev.Fit  Residual   St.Resid
 30      3.00      6.000    3.623     0.385     2.377       2.11R
 36      4.00      4.000    1.794     0.523     2.206       2.06R
 56      3.00      1.000    3.415     0.404    -2.415      -2.16R

R denotes an obs. with a large st. resid.
```

The first part of the output is the regression equation. This is the best estimate of what combination of the predictor variables gives the most accurate prediction of the craving score. To predict a given value of the craving score from known values of the smoking motivation scores one substitutes these values in the equation, multiplying them by their weights (-.181 in the case of C14) and adding the resulting values together with the constant (2.66).

You are given the Multiple R Squared (R-sq), and the adjusted Multiple R squared (R-sq (adj)). The latter tells you the proportion of variance in the dependent variable that is accounted for by the combined predictor variables. You are also given a table of regression coefficients, t-values and their significance levels. Those with significance levels of less than .05 can be said to make a significant contribution to predicting the dependent variable **even once the contributions of all the other designated predictor variables have been taken into account.**

The final part of the output consists of a table of cases which either do not fit well with the predicted values of craving given the values of the predictor variables or have by virtue of their extremity on one or more variables unduly affected the regression. It is not clear how best to deal with these cases. They cannot reasonably be deleted from the analysis unless there are other grounds for considering that they are spurious. However, their presence may invalidate the assumptions under which the multiple regression is carried out and should lead the results to be viewed with caution.

Stepwise multiple regression

To carry out a stepwise multiple regression on the same data you would type the command:

```
MTB>    STEPWISE C2 C14-C20
```

The format of the command is very similar to the forced entry multiple regression command except that you do not have to specify the number of variables in the list of designated predictors.

The results of this command are shown below. After the step 1 there is a single variable (C20) entered into the regression equation with a regression coefficient (weight) of .365 and a t-value of 4.99 (this is significant at p<.05 although not stated in the output). The R squared is 31.55 which means that 31.55 percent of the variance in the craving score is accounted for by the single variable C20 (smoking to relieve craving). At step 2, there are two variables which contribute independently to the prediction of craving. C20 still predicts craving and in fact the t-value is slightly greater indicating a closer relationship once the other independent predictor, C15, has been included in the regression equation. The t-value corresponding to the predictive power of C15 is -3.352 which indicates a negative relationship. Although not stated in the output the t-value of 3.52 is significant at $p<.05$; if it were not, this variable would not have been entered into the equation. The weights of C20 and C15 after step 2 are 3.71 and -1.86 respectively. The constant of the regression equation is 2.405.

```
STEPWISE REGRESSION OF    C2    ON  7 PREDICTORS, WITH N =    56

     STEP        1        2
CONSTANT     1.738    2.405

C20          0.365    0.371
T-RATIO       4.99     5.57

C15                  -0.186
T-RATIO              -3.52

S            1.30     1.18
R-SQ        31.55    44.49
  MORE? (YES, NO, SUBCOMMAND, OR HELP)
```

The fact that the process did not continue beyond step 2 indicates that no further variables made significant independent contributions to the prediction of craving.

The output ends with a question as to whether you want to issue some subcommands or end the stepwise regression. Normally you would type NO followed by a press on the Enter key to indicate that you have finished the analysis.

11.4 Conclusion

This chapter has explained how to carry out forced entry and stepwise multiple regression analyses using SPSS and MINITAB. Multiple regression can be a very powerful tool. It allows you to some extent to make up for the limitations of correlational designs by assessing the extent to which individual variables are associated with a dependent variable independently of association with other variables.

However, there are some major limitations to this technique which you should bear in mind. If two or more of your predictor variables are highly correlated with each other, then in a forced entry multiple regression they may cancel each other out in predicting a dependent variable so that neither comes out as a significant independent predictor. In a stepwise multiple regression one will be entered at the expense of the other even though the difference in predictive power between then is minimal - thus which one of them enters the equation is merely a matter of chance.

Besides this, you must remember that only linear associations are being examined and no-account is taken of interactions between predictor variables. It is possible in theory to cope with these complexities but the methods used bring in a new set of problems.

In the end, the fact remains that you are dealing with correlational data in which there is likely to be some confounding of variables. Thus the results of multiple regression, like any other correlational technique cannot unequivocally indicate direct or causal links between variables. The only secure way to do this is to conduct an experiment in which variables are manipulated independently and the effects observed.

Chapter 12

Factor analysis

12.1 About factor analysis

Factor analysis is a technique for finding a small number of underlying dimensions from among a larger number of variables. For example, it was used initially to find a dimension of intelligence underlying a large number of individual test scores. It has also been used to find a small number of personality dimensions (e.g. extraversion) from answers to a large number of self-report questions.

There are generally two steps to a factor analysis: the **extraction** of the factors and the **rotation** of the factors. The former finds out how many dimensions there are, and the latter obtains a clearer picture of what these dimensions (or factors) represent.

Factor extraction

There are many methods of factor extraction and they often give similar though not identical results. Most common is extraction of **principal components**. This is not strictly speaking a factor analysis. It works by performing a regression analysis on the variables, working out first of all the regression line which best fits all the data points. This first regression line is the first principal component. Then the differences between scores on each variable and the nearest point on the regression line are calculated and a second regression is performed on these differences (otherwise known as **residuals**). This forms the second principal component. This is repeated until there are as many principal components as there are variables.

If the scores on the variables can be reduced to a smaller number of underlying dimensions, only a small number of these principal components will be meaningful.

Exactly what constitutes a meaningful component and where to draw the line is a matter of judgement (rather like the .05 level in significance tests). However certain conventions have emerged. One of these is that a principal component should explain or account for a reasonably large proportion of the variance in all the original variables. This is indicated by its having an **eigenvalue** greater than 1. (Eigenvalues are indices of how much variance in the original set of variables a factor or principal component accounts for.)

Another is that if you plot the eigenvalues of the principal components on a graph with component number (first, second, third etc.) on the X axis and the eigenvalue of each on the Y axis, those components above the **point of inflection** are deemed meaningful and those below are not. This is known as the **scree plot** method. More about all this later.

Note: A point of inflection is where in a curve the slope undergoes a noticeable change.

The most commonly used method of "true" factor extraction is the **maximum likelihoods** method. I will not explain how this works because it is far less easy to understand in non-mathematical terms than extraction of principal components. Suffice it to say that similar criteria can be used to determine the number of meaningful factors as were used with principal components analysis. However, the popularity of the maximum likelihoods approach stems from the fact that you can also use a standard significance test to assess to what extent a given number of factors accounts for the variance in the variables being analyzed. More on this later.

Factor rotation

There are two main classes of factor rotation method: **orthogonal** and **non-orthogonal**. Once a set of common factors has been identified, there remains the question of how the individual variables relate to those common factors.

In an ideal world each variable would relate very strongly to only one factor. Thus factor 1 might have three or four variables which related to it, factor 2 might have another three or four and so on. In the real world, things are never that simple. Any given variable might relate to two or more factors. Factor rotation is a method by which the relationships between variables and factors can be adjusted so as to fit most closely the ideal situation. This may seem a bit of a fix, but it merely reflects the fact that factor analysis is an indeterminate process with literally an infinite number of outcomes which mathematically fit the data - the trick is to find the one which makes most sense from a research point of view.

Relationships between variables and factors are indexed by correlation coefficients, otherwise known as **factor loadings**.

Orthogonal rotation methods make the assumption at the outset that the factors are completely independent of each other - they are not correlated in any way. For example, extraversion and neuroticism dimensions of the Eysenck Personality Questionnaire are supposed to be independent factors. The most commonly used orthogonal rotation method is **varimax** rotation.

In case you are interested, this works by maximizing the variance of the factor loadings for a given variable within the permitted constraints. This has the effect of going as far as it is possible to go in making one or two factor loadings high and the others low.

Non-orthogonal rotation methods allow for the possibility that the factors may be correlated with each other. For example, verbal and spatial IQ are supposed to be separable but related factors. The most often used non-orthogonal rotation technique is **oblimin**. I won't explain how this works because it is hard to describe in non-mathematical terms. The result is a set of factor loadings and also a table of estimated correlations between the factors.

Given the options available for extraction and rotation, you will need some guidance on which method to use when. Sadly, there are no hard and fast rules. You could try the following:

Rule 1
If your purpose is no more than to "reduce the data" to manageable proportions, you should use a principal components analysis. Reducing the data means taking a large number of variables and seeing whether they can be combined to produce a smaller number of variables which can be treated in essentially the same way. It does not matter whether factors produced have any theoretical validity.

Conversely, if you are trying to discover psychologically meaningful underlying dimensions you should try a maximum likelihood factor analysis.

Rule 2
If your purpose is data reduction or you have theoretical reasons to suppose that the underlying dimensions should be unrelated, then you should use an orthogonal rotation method. If you do not know whether or not the underlying factors might be correlated, and it makes a difference to your theory, then you should try a non-orthogonal rotation method first. If the correlations between the factors turn out to be very low, you could re-do the factor analysis with an orthogonal rotation method.

The results of a factor analysis include:

1.   a **list of factors** accepted as being meaningful, each with an eigenvalue and a figure representing the proportion of variance in the original set of variables that it accounts for.

2.   a **rotated factor matrix** which is merely a table of correlations between the variables and the factors (factor loadings).

3.   If you have carried out a maximum likelihood factor analysis, you will also have a **Chi-square** statistic and significance value. If the significance value is less than .05 then the factors you have extracted do not really provide an adequate account of the original variables. You may need to permit the extraction of more factors by relaxing the criterion used for defining whether a factor is meaningful (see below for how to do this).

4.   If you have used an oblimin rotation method, you will be presented with a **structure matrix** and a **pattern matrix**. The structure matrix indicates the correlations between variables and factors but these may be contaminated by correlations between factors. The pattern matrix shows the uncontaminated correlations between variables and factors and is generally used for interpreting factors. You will also have a **table of correlations** between the factors. If these correlations are low (less than, say, .2), you might wish to work on the basis that your factors were not correlated after all and do the analysis again using an orthogonal rotation (e.g. varimax).

Once you have the results of your analysis, you have to decide the following:

1.   Do the results genuinely indicate that the data can be reduced to a smaller number of underlying dimensions? Factor analysis will always produce some kind of result - your task is to figure out whether this means anything.

You should not assume, as many do, that because you have carried out a factor analysis, the results have to be interpretable - often they are not. If that is the case, just accept it. Basically, if after rotation you do not have a "clean" factor structure, i.e. you have quite a lot of variables loading to at least a moderate degree on more than one factor, you will have problems of interpretation.

2.   What interpretation can be put on the underlying factors? This is usually done by looking at what variables load highly on each factor and coming up with a label for the factor which reflects the nature of the variables that correlate with it most highly.

Remember, these labels are a construction arising from your own head - depending on your understanding of what has given rise to your data, they may or may not be misleading. The same applies to your reading of factor analyses carried out by other people. Do not be misled into taking other people's factor labels at face value - they may or may not reflect the true nature of an underlying dimension which may or may not exist.

Reporting factor analyses
When reporting the results of a factor analysis, you should always indicate the extraction and rotation method used, the criterion for accepting factors as meaningful, the proportion of variance in the original variables accounted for by all those factors which you have accepted, the rotated factor matrix and the labels you have chosen to give the factors.

12.2 Requirements for carrying out factor analysis

A basic rule of thumb is that you need at least three times as many cases as variables entered into the factor analysis to get anything like a useable result. In fact, even with a ratio much greater than this the results of factor analysis can be subject to a large and indeterminate margin of error. Thus it is not uncommon for different factor structures to emerge from the same set of variables collected on different groups of subjects.

To perform a maximum likelihood factor analysis your variables should be normally distributed. Principal components analysis is less demanding and indeed is often performed on dichotomous variables (which can take on only one of two possible values, e.g. "yes" or "no" on a questionnaire).

If your purpose is to discover underlying dimensions which are supposed to have some psychological reality, the variables you include in the analysis should not be artificially related and should be representative of all the variables to which you wish to generalise. In practice, neither of these conditions are satisfied in most factor analyses you will find in the literature. The former condition means that you should not have several variables which are no more than replications of each other. For example, you could have two items in a questionnaire as follows:

```
How depressed are you?

Very depressed          1
Quite depressed         2
Note very depressed     3
Not at all depressed    4

How miserable are you?

Very miserable          1
Quite miserable         2
Not very miserable      3
Not at all miserable    4
```

These questions are likely to be interpreted by respondents as meaning pretty much the same thing. This will distort the factor structure by construction of a spurious factor which does no more than reflect the fact that you have obtained several measures of the same thing. In doing this, it will tend to mask other, perhaps weaker, factors which reflect genuinely interesting dimensions.

12.3 Exploratory versus confirmatory factor analysis

The factor analytic methods described in the chapter relate to **exploratory factor analysis**. The principal underlying it is that you have a data set and you want to try to make sense of it. This can be contrasted with **confirmatory factor analysis** in which you have a clear idea of what underlying factor structure you are looking for and you want to examine how far the data are consistent with that structure. SPSS does not have facilities for carrying out confirmatory factor analysis. However, your computer might have a program called LISREL which will perform this analysis. LISREL can actually be run using SPSS. It is available in both mainframe and PC versions. If you think you need a confirmatory factor analysis, you should make enquiries from your computer centre.

After this brief guide to factor analysis, here is how to do it.

12.4 Factor analysis using SPSS

Suppose that you wished to see to what extent the scores on the smoking motivation questionnaire in EXAMPLE.DAT could be accounted for by a smaller number of underlying dimensions, you could perform a factor analysis as follows:

SPSS-X> FACTOR VAR=PSY TO ADD.

The results of this are shown below.

```
Extraction  1  for Analysis  1, Principal-Components Analysis (PC)

Initial Statistics:

Variable    Communality  *  Factor   Eigenvalue   Pct of Var   Cum Pct
                         *
PSY          1.00000     *    1       1.73291        24.8        24.8
HAND         1.00000     *    2       1.29160        18.5        43.2
INDUL        1.00000     *    3       1.06034        15.1        58.4
SED          1.00000     *    4        .91652        13.1        71.4
STIM         1.00000     *    5        .75511        10.8        82.2
AUTO         1.00000     *    6        .68414         9.8        92.0
ADD          1.00000     *    7        .55938         8.0       100.0

    PC Extracted    3 factors.

Factor Matrix:
              FACTOR  1      FACTOR  2      FACTOR  3

PSY            .23114         .74137        -.41071
HAND           .56667         .49318        -.00272
INDUL          .14358         .20686         .91186
SED            .70209        -.14715         .12449
STIM           .66373        -.22221        -.04041
AUTO           .60645        -.19305        -.09933
ADD            .19107        -.58961        -.18209
```

```
Final Statistics:
Variable      Communality  *  Factor   Eigenvalue  Pct of Var  Cum Pct
                           *
PSY              .77175    *    1        1.73291      24.8        24.8
HAND             .56435    *    2        1.29160      18.5        43.2
INDUL            .89490    *    3        1.06034      15.1        58.4
SED              .53008    *
STIM             .49155    *
AUTO             .41492    *
ADD              .41731    *
```

Varimax   Rotation 1, Extraction 1, Analysis 1 - Kaiser Normalization

   Varimax converged in   5 iterations.

Rotated Factor Matrix:

```
                FACTOR  1      FACTOR  2      FACTOR  3

PSY             -.02294        .85922        -.18153
HAND             .36734        .62836         .18592
INDUL            .04502       -.01796         .94475
SED              .70764        .05551         .16197
STIM             .70052        .02066        -.01977
AUTO             .63810        .04513        -.07553
ADD              .38254       -.42391        -.30210
```

Factor Transformation Matrix:

```
                FACTOR  1      FACTOR  2      FACTOR  3

FACTOR  1        .94130        .31805         .11317
FACTOR  2       -.33684        .90714         .25225
FACTOR  3       -.02243       -.27556         .96102
```

You can see that by default, SPSS has chosen to carry out a principal components analysis with a varimax rotation. You will also notice that factors are accepted as meaningful if their eigenvalues are greater than 1.

The first part of the output consists of a table of the factors extracted, their eigenvalues and percentage variance in the total set of variables which each one accounts for. The variable list on the left hand side is not relevant and can be ignored. The table states that the first factor accounted for 24.8 percent of the variance, the second accounted for 18.5 percent and the third accounted for 15.1 percent. Only the first three factors have eigenvalues greater than 1 and so by default only these three are considered meaningful. Between them they account for 58.4 percent of the variance in the original variables. This is fairly typical but you should be aware that this means that a substantial amount of the variation in the original variables remains unaccounted for. This may reflect measurement error or noise, or it may reflect the fact that the variables are not in fact all that closely related to each other.

The factor matrix table is generally ignored unless there is only one factor extracted. It is a table of correlations between the variables and the factors extracted before any factor rotation has taken place. If there is only one factor then there can be no rotation and the "factor loadings" in the factor matrix can be used to determine the labelling of the factor and to see which variables most closely relate to that factor. If there are two or more factors then this analysis should be applied to the rotated factor matrix given later in the output.

The table of "final statistics" re-iterates the eigenvalues and percentage variance accounted for by the three factors which have been accepted as meaningful. It also gives a column of "communalities" for the variables. The communality of a variable represents the extent to which it can be explained by some combination of the three factors.

The rotated factor matrix gives the correlations (loadings) between the variables and the factors after varimax rotation. The first factor has high loadings for SED (smoking for a calming effect), STIM (smoking to increase arousal level) and AUTO (smoking without thinking about it). It may therefore reflect smoking motivation linked to nicotine intake because nicotine is purported to have sedative and stimulant actions. The automatic smoking aspect may be a byproduct of these smoking motives. The second factor has high loadings for the non-pharmacological aspects of smoking, PSY (psychological image) and HAND (the manipulation of the cigarette). The third factor has a high correlation with a single variable, INDUL (smoking for pleasurable relaxation).

Notice that ADD (smoking to relieve craving) loads to a moderate degree on all three factors. This means that craving is partially related to all three dimensions of smoking motives. However, the correlation with the second factor is negative suggesting that smoking to relieve craving is inversely related to psychological motives for smoking.

The factor transformation matrix gives the transformation carried out to turn the factor matrix into the rotated factor matrix. It can normally be ignored.

If you had wanted a maximum likelihood factor analysis, with varimax rotation, you would type:

```
SPSS-X> FACTOR VAR=PSY TO ADD / EXTR=ML / ROTAT=VARIMAX.
```

Note: If you specify a maximum likelihood extraction method, you MUST explicitly state the rotation method you want, otherwise SPSS will assume that you don't want one at all.

The relevant parts of the output for this command are given below. The initial statistics table is the same as before. Notice, however, that it is followed by a Chi-square test. If this yields a significant value (p<.05) and the data conform to a multivariate normal distribution, the factors extracted leave the associations between the variables unexplained to a statistically significant degree.

```
Extraction  1  for Analysis  1, Maximum Likelihood (ML)

Initial Statistics:
Variable        Communality  *  Factor    Eigenvalue    Pct of Var    Cum Pct
                             *
PSY                .13362    *    1         1.73291        24.8          24.8
HAND               .16230    *    2         1.29160        18.5          43.2
INDUL              .05527    *    3         1.06034        15.1          58.4
SED                .16166    *    4          .91652        13.1          71.4
STIM               .13897    *    5          .75511        10.8          82.2
AUTO               .11870    *    6          .68414         9.8          92.0
ADD                .05994    *    7          .55938         8.0         100.0

    ML Extracted   3 factors.    6 Iterations required.
Chi-square Statistic:          .3785, D.F.:    3, Significance:      .9446

Final Statistics:

Variable        Communality  *  Factor    Eigenvalue    Pct of Var    Cum Pct
PSY                .99900    *    1         1.07808        15.4          15.4
HAND               .19766    *    2         1.07964        15.4          30.8
INDUL              .99900    *    3          .95757        13.7          44.5
SED                .34065    *
STIM               .28603    *
AUTO               .22209    *
ADD                .07088    *
```

```
Rotated Factor Matrix:
                  FACTOR  1      FACTOR  2      FACTOR  3
PSY                .99595        -.08381        -.00830
HAND               .31138         .12734         .29066
INDUL              .02038         .99915         .01701
SED                .05616         .08141         .57521
STIM               .02547         .00525         .53418
AUTO              -.00663        -.03557         .46987
ADD               -.16308        -.08595         .19207
```

Notice that the final statistics are different from those provided by the principal components analysis described earlier. The proportion of variance accounted for by the three factors is generally less than occurs with principal components analysis. This is because the principal components analysis specifically seeks to explain as much of the variance in the original variables as possible whereas the maximum likelihood method seeks to explain the relationships between the variables (not quite the same thing).

The rotated factor matrix also gives a slightly different result from that obtained with the principal components analysis. Factor 3 corresponds most closely to factor 1 of the principal components analysis; factor 2 corresponds to factor 3 and factor 1 with factor 2. However, the loadings are different and in the case of the present factor 1 there is a high loading only for PSY.

If you had wanted a principal components analysis with oblimin rotation, you would have typed:

SPSS-X> FACTOR VAR=PSY TO ADD / EXTR=PC / ROTAT=OBLIMIN.

As shown below, this rotation methods produces a pattern matrix and a structure matrix instead of the rotated factor matrix. This arises because the factors are potentially correlated with each other using this rotation method. The pattern matrix gives the correlations between variables and the factors **once any confounding of correlations between factors has been taken into account**. The structure matrix gives the correlations between variables and factors, part of which may arise because a variable correlates with another factor which happens to be correlated with the factor in question. Because the loadings in the pattern matrix are uncontaminated by possible correlations between the factors, these are generally used when interpreting the factors.

The factor correlation matrix shows the correlations between the factors. In this example, they are very low and so it is reasonable to assume that the factors are in fact orthogonal (statistically unrelated to each other) and re-do the analysis using a varimax rotation.

```
    Oblimin converged in    8 iterations.
  Pattern Matrix:

                  FACTOR  1        FACTOR  2        FACTOR  3

  PSY              -.03316          .88391          -.23514
  HAND              .36066          .60883           .15475
  INDUL             .04713         -.11064           .95621
  SED               .70761          .02800           .16901
  STIM              .70052          .01066          -.01262
  AUTO              .63769          .04181          -.07119
  ADD               .38695         -.40445          -.27518


  Structure Matrix:

                  FACTOR  1        FACTOR  2        FACTOR  3

  PSY              -.00712          .84670          -.09825
  HAND              .37527          .64235           .24502
  INDUL             .03415          .03833           .93863
  SED               .70659          .07297           .16592
  STIM              .70094          .02738          -.01833
  AUTO              .63955          .04781          -.07142
  ADD               .37905         -.43665          -.34172


  Factor Correlation Matrix:

                  FACTOR  1        FACTOR  2        FACTOR  3

  FACTOR  1        1.00000
  FACTOR  2         .02666         1.00000
  FACTOR  3        -.01049          .15447          1.00000
```

It is worth observing that the pattern matrix and the structure matrix are very similar. This is because the factors are in fact not highly correlated with each other.

Other criteria for factor extraction
Suppose that you wanted to change the criterion for accepting factors as meaningful. One criterion mentioned at the start of this chapter was to look at the point of inflection on a scree

plot. First obtain a scree plot like this:

SPSS-X> FACTOR VAR=PSY TO ADD / PLOT=EIGEN.

The resulting scree plot is shown below. It looks as though the point of inflection lies between the second and third factors. Thus there is a case for discarding the third factor. This makes a certain amount of sense when one considers that only one variable has a high loading on the third factor and therefore does not do a very good job in reducing the number of dimensions needed to explain the data.

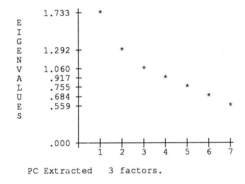

PC Extracted 3 factors.

You could therefore perform the factor analysis again, this time specifying that you only want it to accept two factors.

To perform the factor analysis again limiting it to two factors, you type:

SPSS-X> FACTOR VAR=PSY TO ADD / CRITERIA=FACTORS(2).

This example has assumed that you wanted a principal components analysis with varimax rotation. If you want a maximum likelihood extraction or want to specify a different rotation method, you do so as explained previously.

If you have used a maximum likelihood factor analysis, you can use the Chi-square significance test as a basis for determining the number of factors. To do this you would perform several maximum likelihood factor analyses with different numbers of factors specified. The one with the minimum number of factors whose significance level was **greater than .05** would be chosen.

When things go wrong

Factor analysis does not involve direct calculation of results as do the statistical operations described earlier in this book. It uses what is known as an **iterative** process. This means that the computer works towards the solution in a step by step fashion until, hopefully, it gets near enough as makes no difference.

Unfortunately, sometimes the process gets stuck and no solution can be found. This is particularly common in maximum likelihood extraction and oblimin rotation methods. What will happen is that after a longer than normal pause, the computer will display a message including the words "failed to converge after 25 iterations". It will also indicate whether the problem lay with the extraction or the rotation.

Your first recourse in this event is to allow the computer a few more iterations to find the solution. Suppose that the convergence failed in the extraction, you could increase the permitted number of iterations from the usual 25 to, say, 35 as follows:

```
SPSS-X>  FACTOR VAR=PSY TO ADD/CRITERIA = ITERATE(35) /
CONT>    EXTRACT = ML / ROTATE = OBLIMIN.
```

If the failure to converge is in the rotation then the equivalent command is:

```
SPSS-X>  FACTOR VAR=PSY TO ADD / EXTRACT=ML /
CONT>    CRITERIA=ITERATE(35) / ROTATE=OBLIMIN.
```

Notice that the difference is where you put the CRITERIA command. It applies to the extraction or rotation command which immediately follows it.

If this does not work then your best bet is to try a different extraction or rotation method. Thus if you were using maximum likelihood factor analysis you would have to try a principal components analysis. If the failure to converge occurred during an oblimin rotation, you would have to try a varimax rotation. This is clearly not very satisfactory.

12.4 Conclusion

This chapter has provided a very brief outline of factor analysis and how to carry it out using SPSS. MINITAB has no facilities for factor analysis. It can perform a principal components analysis, but has no facilities for factor rotation so unless there is a single factor solution it is unlikely to be of much use to psychologists.

Factor analysis is now very widely used, and very widely misused. It is not my purpose here to send yet more researchers into the world with a knowledge of how to carry out factor analysis but without knowing how to do so appropriately or interpret the results sensibly. I would advise you to treat factor analysis with utmost caution and to experiment with various methods so that you can get a feel for the instability of the results.

Chapter 13

Cluster Analysis and Discriminant Function analysis

Cluster analysis is a set of exploratory techniques for assessing to what extent and in what way cases may be grouped according to their scores on one or more variables. The extent of clustering is a matter of degree.

Discriminant function analysis examines how well a set of one or more variables can discriminate between two or more groups defined in some way.

13.1 Cluster analysis

Suppose that you wished to know to what extent subjects in EXAMPLE.DAT could be clustered according to their smoking motivation scores. To do this you could type the command:

SPSS-X> CLUSTER PSY TO ADD / PLOT=DEND.

All you would need to change for analyzing your own data are the names of the variables you want to be taken into account. The PLOT=DEND command requests a **dendrogram** display of the results (much more readable than the **icicle plot** which SPSS gives you otherwise).

The results are shown on the following page. This cluster analysis procedure calculates the distance in a seven-dimensional space (there are seven variables) between the cases and agglomerates (combines) the cases step by step until they are all included. The first agglomeration is based on the shortest "euclidean distances" (a spatial analogy in which the data values are assumed to conform to properties of "interval level" measurement) between cases, the second on the next shortest and so on.

Dendrogram using Average Linkage (Between Groups)

Rescaled Distance Cluster Combine

Cases are agglomerated into clusters on the basis of the average distance between the case and mean of the variables already in tch cluster. Two clusters are agglomerated on the basis of the average distance betwcen the means of variables in one cluster and the means of variables in the other. This is known as the method of **average linkage**.

The cases are identified by their **case numbers**. These are not the subject numbers you have given the subjects but numbers automatically assigned to subjects by SPSS **in the order that the cases appear in the data file**. Thus you should make sure that your subject numbers are the same as the case numbers when it comes to interpreting the output so that you know which cases are which.

You should observe that the cluster analysis is **hierarchical**; i.e. any given case is only allowed to belong to one group or cluster at each level. You will also observe that all the cases are ultimately included in the highest level cluster. Thus the level at which you decide that the clusters are meaningful is a matter of judgement.

There are no generally agreed upon statistical tests to help in this. Some researchers perform an analysis of variance on the variables having constructed a new variable which is supposed to represent the presumed clusters. This is tautological and utterly flawed because the clusters have been derived so as to maximize the difference between them. Another method if your data set is large enough is to select various random subsets of the data and perform separate analyses on these. If similar numbers of clusters emerge with similar characteristics (see below), this is indicative of the stability of the clusters. Another alternative is to examine the extent to which group membership based on the cluster analysis discriminates between some external variable. For example, one might examine whether the groups were associated with different prominent withdrawal symptoms during abstinence.

Characterising the clusters

In the above example, it looks as though there are two relatively coherent clusters and a number of subjects who show no affinity to any particular cluster. The first cluster is subject 40 down to 22 and the second cluster is subject 6 down to 43. The subjects below this in the dendrogram fall into several rather disjointed clusters. To characterise the clusters you could create a new SPSS variable containing a number corresponding to the group to which each subject is considered to belong and then use the MEANS command to examine the mean scores of the different groups on each of the variables used in the clustering process.

In the example below, I have used the PRINT=CLUSTER(7) subcommand to provide a printout of what subjects it assigns to what groups on the assumption that there are seven groups or clusters. This is used in conjunction with the SAVE CLUSTER(M) subcommand which asks SPSS to create a new variable containing numbers corresponding to the groups it has assigned each case to.

Note: I chose seven clusters after experimenting with different numbers of clusters. Seven was the smallest number which allowed differentiation of the two main clusters (cases 40 to 22, and cases 6 to 43).

The M tells SPSS to give this new variable the name M followed by a number corresponding to how many clusters were requested (in this case, the number 7). Doing this also requires that I specify explicitly what clustering method is to be used using the METHOD subcommand, and in that command I have also to tell SPSS what the name of the variable containing the group identifiers is to be. Thus the METHOD subcommand is: METHOD=BAVERAGE (M) which means use the method of average linkage (the one which SPSS used before), and use the variable name M to store the group identifiers.

I can then use the MEANS command (see Chapter 5) to obtain the means and standard deviations of the clustering variables. This will enable me to determine the profile corresponding to each cluster.

Here is the complete set of commands:

```
SPSS-X> CLUSTER PSY TO ADD / METHOD=BAVERAGE (M) /
CONT>   PRINT=CLUSTER(7) / PLOT=DEND / SAVE CLUSTER(M).
SPSS-X> MEANS PSY TO ADD BY M7.
```

Below is an extract of the results from the MEANS command in which the means and SDs of the variables PSY, HAND and INDUL are presented. Notice that the two main groups are 2 and 3, as observed graphically in the dendrogram shown earlier. These groups do not differ much on either PSY or INDUL, but they do differ on HAND.

```
Summaries of    PSY
By levels of    M7

Variable        Value  Label              Mean    Std Dev    Cases
For Entire Population                    1.3036    1.6940       56
M7                  1                    1.4000    2.1909        5
M7                  2                    1.6316    1.5352       19
M7                  3                     .6818    1.1291       22
M7                  4                     .0000     .0000        2
M7                  5                     .3333     .5774        3
M7                  6                    4.7500     .9574        4
M7                  7                     .0000     .0000        1
Summaries of    HAND
By levels of    M7

Variable        Value  Label              Mean    Std Dev    Cases
For Entire Population                    3.6786    3.0158       56
M7                  1                     .4000     .5477        5
M7                  2                    5.8947    1.6294       19
M7                  3                    1.5000    1.7113       22
M7                  4                    1.0000    1.4142        2
M7                  5                    8.3333     .5774        3
M7                  6                    6.2500    2.5000        4
M7                  7                    7.0000     .0000        1

Summaries of    INDUL
By levels of    M7

Variable        Value  Label              Mean    Std Dev    Cases
For Entire Population                    4.9286    1.9896       56
M7                  1                    4.8000    2.7749        5
M7                  2                    5.7368    1.8512       19
M7                  3                    4.2727    1.7507       22
M7                  4                    6.0000    4.2426        2
M7                  5                    4.0000    1.0000        3
M7                  6                    4.7500    2.0616        4
M7                  7                    6.0000     .0000        1
```

You may or may not want to interpret the remaining clusters. You should remember that these might represent real clusters which happen not to have many subjects in this sample. Alternatively, they may represent cases that do not fall into any identifiable cluster using the variables contained in the present analysis. If you were to delete these cases, you would not necessarily expect a two-cluster solution to emerge from an analysis of the remaining cases.

Cluster analysis takes quite a long time for the computer to process and you may also find that it is limited in the number of cases that can be handled. On PCs, this is usually around 250.

13.2 Discriminant function analysis

Discriminant function analysis using SPSS

Suppose that you want to know to what extent the craving scores in EXAMPLE.DAT allow you to discriminate between the cases in the four different conditions, you could type the command:

```
SPSS-X> DISCRIM GROUPS=COND(1,4) /VAR=CRAV1 CRAV2
CONT>   CRAV3 CRAV4 /METHOD=DIRECT /STAT=TABLE.
```

In SPSSPC+, the command is slightly different:

```
SPSS/PC:DSCRIM GROUPS = COND(1,4) / VAR=CRAV1 CRAV2
CONT>   CRAV3 CRAV4 /METHOD=DIRECT /STAT=13.
```

Note: The spelling of DSCRIM is not a typing mistake. SPSSPC+ uses that spelling on purpose.

This command tells SPSS to perform a discriminant function analysis to discover the extent to which the four conditions can be discriminated using some combination of the variables CRAV1, CRAV2, CRAV3 and CRAV4. The METHOD command tells SPSS to enter all discriminating variables together. It is similar in this sense to the forced entry method of multiple regression (see Chapter 11). The STAT=TABLE command (or STAT=13 in SPSSPC+) tells SPSS to produce a table showing the proportions of cases correctly and incorrectly classified.

The results of this analysis are shown below. The first part of the output states that SPSS has set a "tolerance" level of .00100. This is to avoid calculation errors when variables entered into the discriminant analysis are very highly correlated with each other. If the tolerance threshold is exceeded, the analysis cannot proceed.

```
On groups defined by COND

Analysis number        1
Direct method:  All variables passing the tolerance test are entered.
      Minimum Tolerance Level.................. .00100

Canonical Discriminant Functions
      Maximum number of functions.............       3
      Minimum cumulative percent of variance...  100.00
      Maximum significance of Wilks' Lambda....  1.0000

Prior probability for each group is  .25000

                    Canonical Discriminant Functions

                   Pct of   Cum  Canonical  After  Wilks'
Fcn Eigenvalue Variance  Pct     Corr     Fcn  Lambda    Chisquare  DF  Sig
                                        :   0   .1339     102.561   12  .0000
 1*    4.1493    90.57   90.57    .8977 :   1   .6893      18.979    6  0042
 2*     .3819     8.34   98.91    .5257 :   2   .9525       2.482    2  .2891
 3*     .0499     1.09  100.00    .2180 :

    * marks the    3 canonical discriminant functions remaining in the
analysis.

Standardized Canonical Discriminant Function Coefficients

               FUNC  1    FUNC  2    FUNC  3
CRAV1         1.00296     .65191    -.69125
CRAV2          .14994    -.86539     .44735
CRAV3         -.11929    -.06090     .86375
CRAV4         -.32133     .71724     .40466

Structure Matrix:


Pooled-within-groups correlations between discriminating variables
                        and canonical discriminant functions

(Variables ordered by size of correlation within function)

               FUNC  1    FUNC  2    FUNC  3
CRAV1          .93838*     .28950     .18576
CRAV2          .62353*    -.36513     .53202
```

```
CRAV4        -.06178      .69850*     .53915
CRAV3         .45699      .09355      .77827*
```

Canonical Discriminant Functions evaluated at Group Means (Group Centroids)

Group	FUNC 1	FUNC 2	FUNC 3
1	2.87050	.05448	.19877
2	.75987	-.06685	-.36251
3	-1.76569	-.83375	.10335
4	-1.86468	.84612	.06040

Classification Results –

Actual Group	No. of Cases	Predicted Group Membership 1	2	3	4
Group 1	14	10 71.4%	4 28.6%	0 .0%	0 .0%
Group 2	14	1 7.1%	12 85.7%	0 .0%	1 7.1%
Group 3	14	0 .0%	1 7.1%	11 78.6%	2 14.3%
Group 4	14	0 .0%	0 .0%	3 21.4%	11 78.6%

Percent of "grouped" cases correctly classified: 78.57%

There are four conditions and so three possible discriminant functions can be computed in theory (always one less than the number of groups or number of cases whichever is the less). These discriminant functions are orthogonal to (independent of) each other. It is possible that anywhere from none to all three functions make independent contributions to classifying the groups.

The prior probability of membership of each group has been set at .25 because there are four groups.

The canonical discriminant functions table is the heart of the output. The column labelled "Percent variance" indicates the percentage of variance in the grouping variable (COND) which is explained by each of the three possible discriminant functions. Notice that the first function explains 90.57 percent of the variance, the second function explains a further 8.34 percent and the third function explains 1.09 percent.

To see whether any or all of the discriminant functions

contribute significantly to classifying the cases into the four conditions look over to the right hand side of the table. Before the first function has been used (After Fcn 0), the groups differ significantly as regards a combination of the values of variables CRAV1 to CRAV4. Thus at least one discriminant function is going to be significant. The Wilks' lambda (an inverse index of discriminative power) is .1339 and the Chi-square statistic derived from this is 102.561 which is highly significant. After the first discriminant function has been entered this reduces to 18.979 which is still significant at p=.0042 so the second discriminant function will also be significant. However, after the second discriminant function has been added the Chi-square is 2.482 with associated p=.2891. We may conclude, therefore, that the first two discriminant functions are useful in classifying cases but that the third is redundant.

The next part of the output which needs to be considered is the structure matrix. This gives the correlations between the variables and the three discriminant functions. This is used to interpret the discriminant functions. You can see that CRAV1 and CRAV2 both correlate highly (.93838 and .62353 respectively) with the first discriminant function. This can therefore be interpreted in terms of craving during the early stages of withdrawal. The second discriminant function is made up mostly of CRAV3 which was a measure of craving after three days.

The final part of the output which needs examining is a classification of the cases according to the discriminant functions. SPSS predicts which group a subject should belong to by calculating which of the calculated mean values of the discriminant functions it is closest to. This classification appears to be reasonably successful and overall is 75.57 percent correct.

Given that the third discriminant function was not significant you can re-do the analysis but only permitting two discriminant functions and then use the classification table based on this analysis. It will be very similar to that shown above but will not include the addition of a small amount of noise added by the third, non-significant discriminant function. The command to do this is:

```
SPSS-X> DISCRIM GROUPS = COND(1,4) / VAR=CRAV1 CRAV2
CONT>    CRAV3 CRAV4 / FUNCTIONS = 2 / METHOD=DIRECT
CONT>    /STAT=TABLE.
```

You can ask SPSS to perform the discrimination function in a stepwise manner, adding variables one by one until they no longer add significantly to the discrimination power. The advantage of this is that you can make sure that only variables which contribute significantly to the discrimination are included in the discriminant function. The command to do this for the data mentioned above is:

```
SPSS/PC:DISCRIM GROUPS=COND(1,4) /VAR=CRAV1 CRAV2
CONT>    CRAV3 CRAV4 /METHOD=WILKS /STAT=TABLE.
```

The only difference is the use of the word WILKS instead of DIRECT. The METHOD=WILKS command tells SPSS to use the WILKS method in a stepwise manner to build up a discrimination function. The results are shown below:

```
---------------- Variables not in the analysis after step   0

                          Minimum
Variable  Tolerance  Tolerance  F to enter   Wilks' Lambda
CRAV1     1.0000000  1.0000000    63.917        .21333
CRAV2     1.0000000  1.0000000    29.090        .37337
CRAV3     1.0000000  1.0000000    15.601        .52629
CRAV4     1.0000000  1.0000000     3.7556       .82192

At step   1, CRAV1   was included in the analysis.

                                 Degrees of Freedom  Signif.
Wilks' Lambda       .21333        1     3     52.0
Equivalent F       63.9167              3     52.0    .0000
---------------- Variables in the analysis after step   1 ----------------

Variable  Tolerance  F to remove  Wilks' Lambda
CRAV1     1.0000000    63.917

---------------- Variables not in the analysis after step   1 -----------

                          Minimum
Variable  Tolerance  Tolerance  F to enter   Wilks' Lambda
CRAV2      .6483402   .6483402     3.3710        .17803
CRAV3      .6561194   .6561194      .83384       .20336
CRAV4      .9324000   .9324000     5.1427        .16379

At step   2, CRAV4   was included in the analysis.

                                 Degrees of Freedom  Signif.
Wilks' Lambda       .16379        2     3     52.0
Equivalent F       25.0059              6    102.0    .0000
```

```
--------------- Variables in the analysis after step   2 ----------------

Variable  Tolerance  F to remove  Wilks' Lambda
CRAV1     .9324000   68.310          .82192
CRAV4     .9324000   5.1427          .21333

--------------- Variables not in the analysis after step   2 ------------

                     Minimum
Variable  Tolerance  Tolerance  F to enter   Wilks' Lambda
CRAV2     .6461687   .6273771   3.1219          .13795
CRAV3     .6435725   .6435725    .75420         .15670

At step   3, CRAV2    was included in the analysis.

                            Degrees of Freedom  Signif.
Wilks' Lambda      .13795      3       3     52.0
Approximate F    17.0133               9    121.8   .0000

--------------- Variables in the analysis after step   3 ----------------

Variable  Tolerance  F to remove  Wilks' Lambda
CRAV1     .6273771   18.961          .29488
CRAV2     .6461687   3.1219          .16379
CRAV4     .9292772   4.8430          .17803

--------------- Variables not in the analysis after step   3 ------------

                     Minimum
Variable  Tolerance  Tolerance  F to enter   Wilks' Lambda
CRAV3     .6188746   .5233645    .49934          .13385

F level or tolerance or VIN insufficient for further computation.

                       Summary Table

             Action     Vars  Wilks'
Step  Entered Removed    In   Lambda   Sig.   Label
  1   CRAV1               1    .21333  .0000
  2   CRAV4               2    .16379  .0000
  3   CRAV2               3    .13795  .0000

                Canonical Discriminant Functions

                   Pct of  Cum  Canonical  After  Wilks'
Fcn Eigenvalue Variance  Pct    Corr      Fcn  Lambda  Chisquare  DF  Sig
                                       :    0   .1379   102.016    9  .0000
 1*   4.1130    90.98   90.98   .8969  :    1   .7053    17.979    4  .0012
 2*    .3811     8.43   99.41   .5253  :    2   .9741     1.351    1  .2451
 3*    .0266      .59  100.00   .1609  :

   * marks the   3 canonical discriminant functions remaining in the
analysis.

Standardized Canonical Discriminant Function Coefficients

          FUNC  1    FUNC  2    FUNC  3
CRAV1     .95378     .62858    -.53771
CRAV2     .12806    -.87473     .87524
CRAV4    -.33544     .71220     .67554

Structure Matrix:

Pooled-within-groups correlations between discriminating variables
                          and canonical discriminant functions
(Variables ordered by size of correlation within function)

          FUNC  1    FUNC  2    FUNC  3
CRAV1     .94251*    .29503     .15696
CRAV3     .53326*    .13498     .28024
CRAV4    -.06195     .70141     .71006*
CRAV2     .62685    -.36011     .69093*
```

The output begins by showing the simple relationship between each of the discriminating variables (CRAV1 to CRAV4) and the grouping variable (COND). This is step 0. The variable whose F-value indicates that it discriminates best between the groups (in a simple one-way analysis of variance) is chosen for entry in step 1. In this case the variable is CRAV1 whose F-value is 63.917. The Wilks' Lambda statistic is an index of the discriminating power of this variable. The smaller the statistic the greater the power.

The next part of the output shows that after step 1, CRAV1 has been entered into the discriminant function analysis. Also provided is a table of variables not yet entered, together with the F-values (F to enter) and Wilks' Lambdas reflecting their ability to add to the discrimination between the groups having taken account of CRAV1 which is already being used. The variable with the highest F to enter will be added to the discriminant function in step 2, but only if the F to enter is above a threshold value indicating that it is statistically significant. In this example, CRAV4 has the highest F to enter and the output in step 2 indicates that this has been duly entered.

After step 2 the variable with the largest F to enter is CRAV2 with an F of 3.1219. This is entered in step 3. After step 3 the only remaining variable not in the discriminant function is CRAV4. However its F to enter is very small indicating that it does not contribute significantly to the discrimination between the groups over and above the function derived from CRAV1 to CRAV3. The process therefore terminates at this point and gives details of the discriminant function with only CRAV1, CRAV2 and CRAV3 in the analysis.

From this point on, you are provided with output similar to that resulting from direct discriminant analysis (in which all the variables are entered together). You may notice that the results in terms of the discriminant functions derived are not the same as were derived from the direct method as shown earlier. The classification table will also be different and in general will probably do less well in correctly classifying the subjects.

However, with the stepwise method one has a clearer indication of the extent to which particular variables contribute to the discrimination process.

Discriminant analysis using MINITAB
MINITAB can be used to perform discriminant function analysis although the output is rather sparse. To perform a discriminant function analysis in which you want to see to what extent the four craving scores (C2, C4, C6 and C8) discriminate between the treatment conditions (C11) you type

MTB>   DISCRIM C11 C2 C4 C6 C8

The first variable mentioned (C11) is always the grouping variable and the remaining variables are the ones used to try to discriminate between the groups.

The main parts of the output are as follows:

```
Linear Discriminant Analysis for C11

Group         1        2        3        4
Count        14       14       14       14

Summary of Classification

Put into      ....True Group....
Group         1        2        3        4
1            10        1        0        0
2             4       12        1        0
3             0        0       11        3
4             0        1        2       11
Total N      14       14       14       14
N Correct    10       12       11       11
Proport.   0.714    0.857    0.786    0.786

N =   56     N Correct =   44      Prop. Correct = 0.786


Squared Distance Between Groups
              1        2        3        4
1        0.0000   4.7845  22.2923  23.0677
2        4.7845   0.0000   7.1836   7.9006
3       22.2923   7.1836   0.0000   2.8336
4       23.0677   7.9006   2.8336   0.0000
```

The Summary of Classification table shows how many subjects were correctly classified using the best possible linear combination of the predictor variables. The next table, the Squared Distance Between Groups, gives the differences between the mean scores of each group on the discriminant function (the combination of the four predictor variables which gives the best discrimination between the groups). You can see that groups 3 and 4 are rather similar and differ a great deal from group 1. Group one differs to a moderate degree from group 2 which differs to a moderate degree from groups 3 and 4. No indication is provided regarding the statistical significance of these differences.

The MINITAB output is too limited to enable its DISCRIM procedure to be used seriously. However, in combination with an analysis of variance it could be used to show how successfully the dependent variable discriminates between the groups.

13.3 Conclusion

This chapter is the last of the chapters on statistical operations. The techniques described are not used all that often in Psychology, but they can be helpful. Cluster analysis can be used to determine to what extent individuals can be separated into non-overlapping groups. In cases where there is reason to believe that there might be discriminable clusters, a grouping variable can be identified in which case a discriminant analysis or analysis of variance may make more sense.

Appendix 1

Using SPSS-X and MINITAB on VAX Computers

This appendix tells you a little about how to use VAX computers which have the VMS operating system.

Registering

If you have not already done so you should now register with the computer centre. This involves obtaining a registration form and following the instructions which go with it.

Once you have registered, you will have a **user name** and **password** (See Chapter 1).

Logging on

To begin a session with the VAX, you sit down at a terminal (see Chapter 1). If necessary you turn it on. Then you press the Enter key once or twice until you are prompted to type in your user name.

After you have typed in your user name (don't forget to press the Enter key at the end of the line), you will be prompted for your password. After you have typed in your password (and pressed Enter) you will have **logged on**.

You will know when you have logged on because you will see the **system prompt** on the left of the screen. This takes the form of a dollar sign.

$

Note: Your terminal may not be connected directly to the VAX. It may be connected to a switching system. If so, you will not be prompted directly for your user name. You might instead see a prompt like this:

PAD>

In that case you will have to enter a command to indicate which of several possible computers you wish to use. This might involve typing a command such as:

PAD> CALL VAX

The command you need may be different. Your computer centre will be able to tell you. Once you have typed such a command, you should be prompted for your user name.

Commands you can use when you see the system prompt
Whenever you see the system prompt on the screen, and your flashing cursor is located immediately after it you know you can type one of these commands:

EDIT
DIR
PRINT
DELETE
PURGE
COPY
LOGOUT

and either

SPSS
or
MINITAB

You should note that there may be all kinds of things on the screen at any one time. For example, there may be commands which you have previously typed in and executed. These will always be above the line that the flashing cursor is on. The important line is the one which the flashing cursor is on, the **current line**.

Note: You can only type commands on the current line. Do not use the cursor keys to move around the screen.

If you make a mistake on a line and have already pressed Enter, the chances are that the computer will display some kind of error message. If it displays the system prompt with the flashing cursor next to it afterwards, you can just type the command in again. If you have accidentally gone into the EDITOR, SPSS or MINITAB (see below), you will have to exit from these packages to get back to the system prompt (how to do this is described below).

When you want to finish a session
At any time when you see the system prompt ($) and the flashing cursor next to it, you can finish your session. You do this by typing:

$ LOGOUT

You must log out at the end of every session (see Chapter 1).

Creating a data file
Now suppose that you have some data that you want to analyze. The very first thing you will have to do is to create a file to store this data.

This is done using the **EDIT** command.

To try out the examples used in this book, you will have to create a file called **EXAMPLE.DAT** which contains the data shown in Appendix 4. To do this, you should type the command:

```
$    EDIT EXAMPLE.DAT
```

You will now see a * on the screen.

You should type C, then press Enter:

```
*    C
```

The screen will go blank. The computer is now waiting for you to type in your data. When you type in the data, make sure that you have at least one space between each variable and that the columns of numbers line up.

The file must contain nothing but numbers.

At the end of each line of data you must press the Enter key to begin a new line.

If you make a mistake, you can use the cursor keys (the four keys with arrows on, located together) to move to the point where you made the mistake and then use the Backspace key (see Chapter 1) to rub out the incorrect characters. Then just type in the correct characters.

Note: The Backspace key rubs out the character just to the left of it. If you have pressed Enter accidentally and want to rub it out, move the cursor to the first character on the next line and press Backspace.

When you have typed in your data, press and hold down the **Control** key (see Chapter 1) and then press **Z** once. There is no need to press Enter.

You should now see a * on the screen. Now type **EXIT** and press Enter. After a while you will see the $ again which means that your file has been stored safely on the magnetic disc.

Note: Your computer might have an editor called **EVE** instead of, or as well as, **EDIT**. EVE is a much more powerful editor, designed to be able to be used for writing essays, reports or papers as well as creating data files.

To begin an edit with EVE in which you want to create or amend a file called EXAMPLE.DAT, you type:

```
$    EVE EXAMPLE.DAT
```

If you are creating the file, the screen will go blank except for a line of information at the bottom of the screen.

You can then type in your data as you would with EDIT. You can use the cursor keys to move around the screen and use the Backspace key to make corrections. You should press Enter to end each line.

When you have finished and you want to save what you have done, you press Ctrl-Z (hold down the Control key and press Z once). This will save EXAMPLE.DAT and put you back to the system prompt ($).

If you want to exit from EVE without it saving anything (i.e. you want to abandon the edit session without having made any changes), you press the F4 key (this might be labelled PF4 on a keypad to the right of your keyboard), and then type QUIT and press Enter.

Amending a data file

Once you have created a file, it is a simple matter to amend or add to it. Let us suppose that you notice that you have made a mistake in your data file, EXAMPLE.DAT. In response to the system prompt ($), you type the command:

```
$    EDIT EXAMPLE.DAT
```

Then you will see an asterisk (*) on the screen. You press **C** followed by Enter. The screen will then display the first screen's worth of your data file EXAMPLE.DAT. The cursor will be located at the start of the first line. You can use the cursor keys to move the cursor to the point which you wish to change.

If, for example, you wish to add more subjects to the end of the data file, you move the cursor to the end of the last line, press Enter to start a new line and begin typing the additional data.

Note: I would strongly recommend that if you have a large amount of data to enter, you do it a bit at a time. Enter about 10 subjects' worth and then use CTRL-Z and EXIT to save what you have done. Then go back into EDIT to add a further 10 subjects' worth of data, and so on. The reason is that sometimes the computer can "crash" or you can be called away and forget to save what you have done. In either case, you would not wish to have wasted several hours of work. If you follow my advice, the most you will lose will be about 20 minutes of your time.

If you wish to correct a mistake, you move the cursor to the character after the one you want to change and then press Backspace to rub out the incorrect character. You can then type in the correct one.

When you have finished making the necessary additions or amendments, you hold down the Control key and press Z once.

This will bring back the *. You then type EXIT. This will save the new version of the file and bring back the system prompt ($).

Looking at a data file

You may simply want to see what is in a data file. The easiest way to do this is to use the EDIT command as though you were going to amend it. Just don't make any changes and instead of using EXIT to leave the editor, you use the word QUIT. Thus to view EXAMPLE.DAT once you have created it, you do the following:

```
$       EDIT EXAMPLE.DAT
*       C
```

Then use the cursor keys to move around the file if you need to see a part of it which is not on the screen. Thus if you move the cursor to the bottom of the screen and keep pressing the down cursor key the screen will **scroll** down allowing you to see further down the file.

When you have finished examining the data file, you press Ctrl-Z (see section on creating a data file), then:

```
*       QUIT
```

This will get you back to the system prompt without updating the file. Of course, if you did not make any changes, the file would not have been changed even if you had used EXIT instead of QUIT. However, as you will see in the next section, a new version of the file would have been created which is rather a waste of disc space.

Getting a printout of your data file

It is often helpful to be able to have the contents of your data files printed out on paper so that you can study them (possibly looking for mistakes). To get a printout of EXAMPLE.DAT, you type the command:

```
$       PRINT EXAMPLE.DAT
```

The contents of this file will then be printed on one of the line-printers at the computer centre. You will have to go to the computer centre to pick up the output. This will probably be in a pigeon hole or tray allocated to your user name. The printout will be identifiable as yours because your user name will be printed in very large characters on the front.

Versions of files and listing your files

Every file in your disc space has a **version number**. When you create a new file, it is given the version number **1**. If you amend that file using EDIT, version 1 of that file stays exactly as it was and a new version (version **2**) is created which includes your changes. If you amend it again, then a version **3** is created, and so on.

Unless you tell it otherwise, the computer will always assume that you wish to work on the most recent version of a given file.

The advantage of this way of working is that if you make an amendment to a file which you later discover was a mistake, the old version of the file is still there for you to work on.

You can see what files you have in your disc space by using the DIR command, as in:

```
$      DIR
```

Here is the kind of thing you can expect to see in response to this command:

```
Directory UHJT:[001]

EXAMPLE.DAT;3      EXAMPLE.DAT;2      EXAMPLE.DAT;1
REACTION.DAT;2     REACTION.DAT;1     SURVEY.DAT;1
DECISION.DAT;1
```

It shows that there are seven files present. Each entry consists of the name you have given the file plus a semicolon followed by a version number. Thus there are three versions of EXAMPLE.DAT, two versions of REACTION.DAT and one version each of SURVEY.DAT and DECISION.DAT.

As previously noted, normally you do not need to specify the version number. The computer automatically assumes that you mean the most recent version. However, you can specify the version number if you wish, e.g. by using EXAMPLE.DAT;1 instead of EXAMPLE.DAT.

Using SPSS-X

Once you have created a data file using EDIT, you can go into SPSS-X just by typing the command:

```
$      SPSSX / OUTPUT=RESULTS.RES
```

When you have done this, you will see the SPSS prompt, which is:

```
SPSS-X>
```

This means that the computer is now waiting for you to type in SPSS commands. It is these commands with which most of the rest of this book is concerned.

Note: To execute a command in SPSS-X, you type in the command with a full stop at the end and press the Enter key. If the command does not fit onto a single line, you can press the Enter key to end each line in a convenient place. The last of the lines used in the command must end with a full stop. The prompt you see for continuation lines is CONTINUE>, but I have shortened it in this book to CONT>.

Here is an example:

```
SPSS-X> DATA LIST FILE=EXAMPLE.DAT FREE / SUBNO CRAV1
CONT>   DIFF1 CRAV2 DIFF2 CRAV3 DIFF3 CRAV4 DIFF4.
```

Displaying results

When SPSS-X executes commands which you type in, the results will often not be able to be fitted onto a single screen's worth. After the screen has filled up, new information appearing at the bottom of the screen will cause the screen to scroll up so that you can no longer see information which has gone off the top. To make the display pause so that you can read it, you should press the **NoScroll** key on the keyboard if there is one. If there is no such key you can press **Ctrl-S** (hold down the Control key and press S once).

To restart the display, you press **NoScroll** again or press **Ctrl-Q**.

When you have finished with SPSS-X for the time being, you must exit from it using the command:

SPSS-X> STOP.

This will leave SPSS-X and bring back the system prompt ($).

Notice that the command to go into SPSS-X in the first place included the subcommand / **OUTPUT=RESULTS.RES**. This is not strictly necessary but I strongly recommend it. What it does is to keep a record of all the results that are displayed on the screen during the SPSS-X session in a file called RESULTS.RES. You can then look at or amend this file using EDIT just as you would a data file (see previous sections in this appendix). You can also print it out using the PRINT command. This means that you do not have to worry about noting down the results from the screen as they appear.

You do not have to use RESULTS.RES as your file name. You can use any name you like. In fact, I suggest that you use different names for different sets of results. If you keep using the same name you will just create lots of files with this name and different version numbers, and you will rapidly forget which is which.

Note: I recommend that you always use .RES as the suffix. This will avoid clashes with data files because the latter should always have .DAT as their suffixes.

Using MINITAB

Once you have created the data file you wish to work on, you can go into MINITAB to analyze the data. To do this you type the command:

$ MINITAB

You will then see the prompt:

MTB>

From this point onwards you can use the commands given in the main body of this book.

To execute commands in MINITAB you just type them in and press Enter. Normally, commands will fit on a single line. If they are too long to fit onto a single line you must end each of the intermediate lines with the symbol **&** (ampersand) before pressing Enter. This tells MINITAB that you have not finished the command yet even though you have come to the end of the line. No command may be more than 80 characters long. You can end the intermediate lines anywhere between words. Here is an example:

MTB>   READ 'EXAMPLE.DAT' C1 C2 C3 C4 C5 &
CONT>   C6 C7 C8 C9 C10 C11-C24

When you want to end your MINITAB session for the time being, you type the command:

MTB>   STOP

This will exit from MINITAB and bring back the system prompt.

Housekeeping with your files

There are various useful things which you can do to keep your files in good order.

Once you have edited a file a few times you will have built up several versions of that file. If you decide that you really do not want the old versions of **all** your files you can type the command:

$ PURGE

(Don't forget to press Enter at the end of the command.)

This gets rid of **all** old versions of **all** files in your space.

If you want to delete a single file, say, REACTION.DAT;1, you use the command:

$ DELETE REACTION.DAT;1

Notice that you have to specify the version number whenever you use DELETE. Even if you want to delete the most recent version of the file, you still have to specify the version number. Thus if you had wanted to delete the most recent version of REACTION.DAT and this was version 2, you would have had to type:

$ DELETE REACTION.DAT;2

It is often useful to copy a file so that you can keep one version under one name and a different version which you will amend under a different name. To make a second copy of EXAMPLE.DAT which you will call EXAMPLE2.DAT, you type:

$ COPY EXAMPLE.DAT EXAMPLE2.DAT

It is also sometimes useful to be able to rename files. To change the name of EXAMPLE2.DAT to EXAMPLE3.DAT, you type:

```
$    RENAME EXAMPLE2.DAT EXAMPLE3.DAT
```

Using wild cards in file specifications

Sometimes you want to perform housekeeping operations on several files at once. It is rather tedious to have to do it individually for each file.

You can save yourself a lot of typing by using **wild cards**. The basic rule is that a ***** stands for anything. At the most extreme, if you type:

```
$    DELETE *.*;*
```

you will delete every file in your disc space! Less drastic is:

```
$    DELETE EXAMPLE2.DAT;*
```

This deletes all versions of EXAMPLE2.DAT.

If you wanted to delete all files with the prefix EXAMPLE2, you would type:

```
$    DELETE EXAMPLE2.*;*
```

Wild cards work with most VMS commands. Suppose that you wanted to list those files in your disc space which began with EXAMPLE. You could type:

```
$    DIR EXAMPLE.*
```

Note: You do not need to specify the version numbers. It is only the DELETE command which requires you to indicate version numbers.

Recap

A typical session might involve the following steps:

1. Log on
2. Go into EDIT to create or amend a data file
3. Type in some data or make some changes
4. Leave EDIT to get back to the system prompt
5. Go into SPSS-X or MINITAB and read in data
6. Enter some commands to perform statistical analyses
7. Leave SPSS-X or MINITAB to get back to the system prompt
8. Log off

If you have already created the data file you wish to work on, your session might look like this:

1. Log on
2. Go into SPSS-X or MINITAB and read in data
3. Enter some commands to perform statistical analyses
4. Leave SPSS-X or MINITAB
5. Log off

An example of a session in which some housekeeping operations are performed is:

1. Log on
2. Use DIR to get a listing of your files
3. PURGE old versions of files
4. Go into EDIT to create a new data file
5. Type in some data
6. Leave EDIT to get back to the system
7. Use DIR to get another listing of your files
8. Use PRINT to get a hard copy of the file just created
9. Log off

One of the commonest mistakes which new users make is to forget to get out of the EDITOR or SPSS-X before trying to type in an operating system command. Remember that you must see the flashing cursor next to the system prompt ($) before you can use an operating system command (e.g. LOGOUT, PRINT).

Using on-line help facilities

Both SPSS-X and MINITAB allow you to ask for help about how to type in commands. You use the SPSS-X help facilities as follows:

1. Make sure you are **in** SPSS-X. That is, if you are at the system prompt, type **SPSSX**. You will know when you are in SPSS-X because you will see the SPSS-X> prompt.

2. Type **HELP** then press the Enter key. You will then see the display shown below:

```
HELP

HELP is available for a variety of SPSS-X topics. Most of the topics are the
actual SPSS-X commands that:

        - define and transform data
        - import or export files
        - perform statistical analysis
        - produce reports
        - perform various utility functions.

    Topics that are SPSS-X commands are given in capital letters, such
    as FREQUENCIES, CROSSTABS, DATA LIST, RECODE, COMPUTE.

    HELP is also available on general SPSS-X topics: HELP for items
    such as "running_SPSSX", "interactive_X" and "syntax rules" can be
    found under entries given in lower-case.

    Enter "help_with_help" for instructions on using SPSS-X HELP.

    Additional information available:

    2SLS          ACF          ADD          AGGREGATE   ALSCAL       ANOVA
    ARIMA         ATTACH       AUTORECODE   batch_X     BEGIN        BOX-JENKINS   AREG
    BREAK         BREAKDOWN    CASEPLOT     CCF         CLEAR        CLUSTER
    COMMENT       COMPUTE      CONDESCRIPTIVES          CORRELATIONS              CNLR
    CREATE        CROSSTABS    CURVEFIT     DATA        data_formats              COUNT
    DEFINE        DESCRIPTIVES              DISCRIMINANT             DISPLAY       DATE
    DOCUMENT      DROP         EDIT         ELSE        END          EXECUTE       DO
    DOCUMENT      DROP         EDIT         ELSE        END          EXECUTE       EXPORT
    EXSMOOTH      FACTOR       FILE         file_types  FINISH       FIT          EXPORT
    FREQUENCIES   GET          HELP         help_with_help                        FORMATS
    HILOGLINEAR   IF           IMPORT       INCLUDE     INFO         INPUT
    interactive_X              invocation_line          KEYED        LEAVE        LISREL
    LIST          LOGLINEAR    LOOP         MACRO       MANOVA       MATCH        MATRIX
    MCONVERT      MEANS        memory_mgmt              MISSING      MODEL        MULT
    N             NEW          NLR          NONPAR      NPAR         NPPLOT       NUMBERED
    NUMERIC       ONEWAY       PACF         PARTIAL     PEARSON_CORR              PLOT
    POINT         PREDICT      PRESERVE     PRINT       PROBIT       PROCEDURE
    PROXIMITIES                QUICK        RANK        READ         RECODE       RECORD
    REFORMAT      REGRESSION   release_notes            RELIABILITY               RENAME
    REPEATING     REPORT       REREAD       RESTORE     RMV          running_SPSS-X
    SAMPLE        SAVE         SEASON       SELECT      SET          SHOW         SORT
    SPAWN         SPECTRA      SPLIT        STRING      SUBTITLE     SURVIVAL
    syntax_diff                syntax_rules             SYSMIS       T-TEST       TABLES
    TDISPLAY      TEMPORARY    TITLE        Trends      TSET         TSHOW        TSPLOT
    UNNUMBERED    UPDATE       USE          VALUE       VARIABLE     VECTOR       VERIFY
    WEIGHT        WLS          WRITE        X11ARIMA    XSAVE        XTABS

Subtopic?
```

Notice that you are asked by the prompt "Subtopic?" to tell the computer what SPSS-X command you want help with. Suppose you want help with the ANOVA command. You just type **ANOVA** and then press Enter. This will produce the display shown below:

```
ANOVA
   ANOVA performs analysis of variance for factorial designs.
   _____
  |ANOVA   PRESTIGE BY REGION(1,9) SEX(1,2).                  |
   -----------------------------------------------------------

   The simplest ANOVA command contains one analysis list with a
   dependent variable list and a factor variable list.  Each analysis
   can contain only one BY keyword.

   Additional information available:

   SYNTAX    VARIABLES  MAXORDERS  COVARIATES METHODS    STATISTICS MISSING
   FORMAT
ANOVA Subtopic?
```

You are being prompted by the words "ANOVA Subtopic?" to type in one of the ANOVA subcommands which you may need help on. Suppose that you want help with the COVARIATES subcommand. You simply type **COVARIATES** and then press Enter.

The rule is that you work your way into the details of commands by following the prompts. If you do not want to follow the help prompt, you simply press Enter without typing anything. That will get you to the previous help prompt and ultimately back to the SPSS-X prompt.

You should try this out with a few commands so that you can see how it works.

To use the MINITAB help facilities you need to do the following:

1. Make sure you are in MINITAB. If you are at the system prompt you simply type **MINITAB** and press Enter. You will know that you are in MINITAB when you see the MTB>

prompt.

2. Type **HELP** followed by the command that you need help with. For example, if you want help with the TABLE command, you type:

MTB>   HELP TABLE

This will produce the display shown below:

```
TABLE the data classified by C,...,C

Subcommands:
        MEANS              DATA                TOTPERCENTS
        MEDIANS            N                   CHISQUARE
        SUMS               NMISS               MISSING
        MINIMUMS           PROPORTION          NOALL
        MAXIMUMS           COUNTS              ALL
        STDEV              ROWPERCENTS         FREQUENCIES
        STATS              COLPERCENTS         LAYOUT

The TABLE command prints one-way, two-way and multi-way tables.
The cells may contain counts, percents and statistics from a
chisquare test; they may also contain summary statistics of
associated variables (i.e., any variable which is not used as a
classification variable).  The cells may also contain data.
```

The first part of the display shows you how to type in the command. The words in lower case ("the data classified by") do not have to be typed in when you type the command. "C,...,C" means one or more variables (e.g. C1 C2 C3).

If you want help with one of the subcommands you should type **HELP TABLE** followed by the subcommand. For example, if you wished help with the STATS subcommand, you would type:

MTB>   HELP TABLE STATS

Try things out until you get the idea. If you really get stuck you could try typing:

MTB>   HELP HELP

This provides help with the help facilities available in MINITAB.

Use of "include files" in SPSS-X and MINITAB

You do not have to read this section but it could save you a great deal of time.

Suppose that you have a lot of commands that you want to execute. You could type them in and execute them one at a time. If you make a mistake at some point, however, you may have to type the whole lot in again. You could save yourself time in the long run if you were to put all the commands into a file and then tell SPSS-X or MINITAB to go to that file and execute any commands it finds there. Files like this, which contain commands to SPSS-X or MINITAB are called **include files** or **run files**. This is how you create them and use them.

Let us create a file called EXAMPLE.RUN containing a set of commands to SPSS-X and then execute those commands.

To create EXAMPLE.RUN, you go into the editor by typing:

```
$      EDIT EXAMPLE.RUN
```

This begins a session editing a file called EXAMPLE.RUN. You will then see a *. Press C then Enter.

Now you can type some commands into the file. Type the following lines (with Enter at the end of each one).

```
DATA LIST FILE = EXAMPLE.DAT FREE / SUBNO
 CRAV1 DIFF1 CRAV2 DIFF2 CRAV3 DIFF3 CRAV4 DIFF4
 SEX COND AGE CO BREATH PSY HAND INDUL
 SED STIM AUTO ADD DEPEND CIGSPD MOTIV TROUB.
MISSING VALUES CRAV1 TO DIFF4 SEX (9) AGE CO
 CIGSPD (99).
SAVE OUTFILE='EXAMPLE.SYS'.
DESCR VAR=CRAV1 CRAV2 CRAV3 CRAV4.
MEANS CRAV1 CRAV2 CRAV3 CRAV4 BY SEX.
```

Now you press Ctrl-Z (Hold down the Control key and press Z once). Then type EXIT and press the ENTER key.

Note: When commands spill over onto more than one line, the **continuation** lines (after the first line), all have to begin with a space.

You will now see the $ prompt again. You will have created a file called EXAMPLE.RUN containing a set of SPSS-X commands. Do not worry about what these commands mean for the present. This will become clear as you go through the book.

The same applies to include files for use with MINITAB except that the commands would be different. You could try typing the following commands into a file:

```
READ 'EXAMPLE.DAT' C1-C24
CODE (9) '*' C2-C11
CODE (99) '*' C12 C13 C22
DESCR C2 C4 C6 C8
TABLE C10;
STAT C2 C4 C6 C8.
```

To execute the commands in EXAMPLE.RUN containing SPSS-X commands, you go into SPSS-X by typing:

```
$       SPSSX
```

Now you type:

```
SPSS-X> INCLUDE EXAMPLE.RUN.
```

Do not forget to type the full stop at the end and press Enter.

You will then see the commands being executed automatically. (The command will only work if you have already created a data file called EXAMPLE.DAT as described earlier in this appendix.)

You can then type further commands directly into SPSS-X, execute another "include file" or exit from SPSS-X using the STOP command as already described.

If you typed the MINITAB commands into EXAMPLE.RUN, to execute these you go into MINITAB by typing:

$ MINITAB

Then you type the command:

MTB>   EXECUTE 'EXAMPLE.RUN'

(Don't forget to press Enter at the end.)

You will then see the commands being executed. When this has finished you can type in further commands, execute another "include file" (if you have one), or exit from MINITAB as described earlier in this appendix.

Amending an "include file"
You can amend an "include file" in the same way as you would amend data files. Suppose that you wanted to amend EXAMPLE.RUN, you would type:

$ EDIT EXAMPLE.RUN

Then press C and Enter. You will see the contents of the file on the screen. You can use the cursor keys to move to the point which you want to change and the Backspace key to delete unwanted characters. Then you can type in any new characters.

To finish the editing session, you press Ctrl-Z and then type EXIT and press Enter.

Conclusion
This appendix has provided an introduction to the use of VAX VMS and how to run SPSS-X and MINITAB analyses using

this operating system. VMS is a very powerful operating system and there are many features not covered in this appendix which you would find useful. Once you have gained some confidence using the simple commands listed here, you should ask your computer centre to provide you with their documentation of VMS. In particular, the text editor (either EDIT or EVE) which you will be using has commands for deleting whole lines, copying text from one place to another and moving text around. This can be very helpful when creating data or command files.

To see complete SPSS-X and MINITAB sessions, turn to Appendix 3.

Appendix 2

Using SPSSPC+ and MINITAB on PCs

In order to know how to run SPSSPC+ and MINITAB on PCs you need to know a little about the machines you are working with, and their operating system, MSDOS. You may need to refer back to Chapter 1 to refresh your memory about PC hardware.

A2.1 MSDOS

MSDOS (Microsoft Disc Operating System) is the most commonly used operating system on PCs. It is essentially the same as PCDOS (in case you use a computer with this operating system).

The system prompt

When you turn the computer on, there is a short delay while the computer **boots up**. This involves it starting up the operating system. Then you will see the **system prompt**. This will normally consist of a **letter** followed by a **colon**, a **backslash**, and a **right angled bracket** intended to represent a right facing arrow (e.g. A:\> or C:\>). Depending on how the system is set up there may also be other text before the right arrow (e.g. C:\SPSS>).

This prompt means that MSDOS is waiting for a command. The flashing cursor next to the arrow indicates where the command will appear on the screen when you type it in.

Disc drive designation

The operation of MSDOS centres on the various disc drives that you may have on the PC. Most PCs have a floppy disc drive which is designated by **A:** and a hard disc which is designated by **C:**. If there is a second floppy disc drive this is usually labelled **B:**, and if there is a second hard disc drive, this is usually labelled **D:**. There may be even more disc drives labelled **E:**, **F:** or **G:**.

The hard disc (and occasionally the floppy disc), will normally be divided into a number of **directories** and **sub-directories**. These are hierarchical in that there is a single **root** directory for the disc as a whole; subsumed under this may be several directories; subsumed under each of these may be several sub-directories, and so on. This is shown schematically below:

```
\
├──DOS
├──HG
├──MOUSE1
├──WIN386
│    └──PIF
├──WP51
└──XTGOLD
```

In this example, under the root directory (\) there are six directories (DOS, HG, MOUSE1, WIN386, WP51 and XTGOLD), and under the WIN386 directory there is a single sub-directory, PIF.

Being "in" directories and "on" discs

From the moment when the machine is switched on, MSDOS puts you **in** one of the directories **on** one of the discs. This means that unless you tell it otherwise, MSDOS will assume that you are dealing with files **in** the **current** directory and **on** the current disc. Files on other discs or in other directories will be invisible to MSDOS **unless you actually specify the directory or disc where they are located.**

You can tell what disc you are on by the prompt which the computer is displaying. If the prompt contains A: you are on the floppy disc drive (or one of them, if you have two); if the prompt contains C: you are on the hard disc (or one of them).

You may or may not be able to tell what directory you are in depending on how the system has been set up. If the system has been set up in a user-friendly manner then the prompt should indicate what directory you are in. On my computer the prompt looks like this when I am in the SPSS directory on drive C:

```
C:\SPSS>
```

and like this when I am in the WP51 directory

```
C:\WP51>
```

For the sake of simplicity, I will just use A:\> or C:\> as the system prompts in examples.

Files

Remember that everything on the discs is stored in files. These files may contain data, programs, documents etc.. SPSS is stored on the hard disc usually in a directory called SPSS and consists of over 20 files. Check back with Chapter 1 if you are unsure about files and file names.

Moving between discs and directories

To move from one disc drive to another you type in the letter corresponding to that drive followed by a colon. Note that you can only do this when the flashing cursor is next to the system prompt - i.e. you are in the MSDOS operating system (as opposed to SPSS or an editor).

For example, if you are on drive A:, and you wish to switch to drive C:, you type the command:

```
A:\>    C:
```

Note: Don't forget to press the Enter key at the end of the line. Also don't forget the convention used in this book that text in italics refers to the prompt that the computer gives you. The text that follows it is what you are supposed to type in.

To move to the directory you want to be in, you use the **CD** command (standing for "Change Directory"), as in:

c:\>   CD \SPSS

This moves you from whatever directory you happened to be in to the SPSS directory (assuming you have one).

If you then wished to move to the MINITAB directory (assuming you have one), you would type:

c:\>   CD \MINITAB

The backslash (\) is necessary in every case when you use the command.

If you wished to go to the root directory (the top level directory on the disc), you would type:

c:\>   CD \

If you ask to move to the directory you are already in, MSDOS will ignore the command. If you ask to move to a directory that does not exist on your current disc, MSDOS will display an error message.

The PATH command

Often the PC has been set up so that you do not actually need to use the CD command to run a program in a particular directory. A **path** will already have been created so that programs in commonly used directories can be run no matter what directory you are currently in on the hard disc.

To find out whether a PATH command has been used, you should type the command:

```
c:\>    PATH
```

This will display whatever paths have been entered already. You might see a display like that shown below:

```
PATH=\WIN386;\MOUSE1;\DOS;\WP51;\XTGOLD;\HG
```

This indicates that there are paths to the WIN386, MOUSE1, DOS, WP51, XTGOLD and HG directories so that you can use any program in one of those directories without actually moving to it first.

If you are at all unsure about what you are doing, you should behave as though there were no PATH command and move to the directory of the program you want to use before you try to use it.

Windows, menus and other user interfaces

Some computers will have been set up so that you do not even need to use MSDOS - you simply go straight into SPSSPC+ or use a menu system to choose from a fixed set of programs to run. Other computers may use a system called **Windows** which allows you to run programs by selecting them from a screen display. If your computer has one of these **user interfaces** other than straightforward MSDOS, you will probably need to get some help from the person who set it up.

Obtaining lists of what files are where

To find out what files there are in the directory you are currently in, just type:

```
c:\>    DIR
```

To find out what files are on a disc in the A: drive when you are on the C: drive, you type:

c:\>   DIR A:

Otherwise you could move to the A: drive by typing **A:** (followed by Enter), and then just type the command DIR.

To find out what is in the \SPSS directory on the C: drive (assuming there is such a directory and you are already on the C: drive), you type:

c:\>   DIR \SPSS

Alternatively, you could move to the \SPSS directory using CD \SPSS and then just type DIR.

To obtain a list of files in the root directory of the C: drive you could type:

c:\>   DIR \

Alternatively you could move to this directory using **CD ** and then just type **DIR.**

In general, to obtain a list of files in a particular directory on a particular disc you either specify the disc and/or directory in the DIR command itself, or else you move to the disc and directory and just type DIR.

On the next page is a typical directory-listing of a root directory on a C: drive obtained by typing DIR \ Notice that there are some files listed as well as some directories. The files are listed using the prefixes and suffixes (e.g. DM.EXE). The directories are listed by the directory name followed by <DIR>. The third column indicates how many bytes are taken up by each file (e.g. DM.EXE takes up 95,568 bytes). The fourth column shows the date when the file was created or last amended and final column shows the time when it was created or amended (a means a.m. and p means p.m.).

The last line indicates that there are 10,737,664 bytes unused on the disc (just over 10 MB). There will be occasions when error messages appear because you have run out of disc space, either on the hard disc or a floppy disc. In that case you may need to delete some unwanted files. It is advisable to keep track of how much space you have left on your discs to pre-empt this.

```
DM        EXE      95568    7-05-89   12:00p
DMDRVR    BIN       8442    7-05-89   12:00p
ONLINE    HLP      33578    7-05-89   12:00p
DOS             <DIR>       3-24-90    6:18p
KEYB      COM      10868    9-16-87   12:00p
KEYBOARD  SYS      41144    9-16-87   12:00p
AUTOEXEC  BAT        218    7-24-90    9:44a
MOUSE1          <DIR>       3-27-90    9:12a
W         BAT         21    7-26-90    8:50a
CONFIG    SYS         48    5-29-90    9:41a
WIN386          <DIR>       4-12-90   12:22p
WINDOWS          256986    4-19-90    6:29p
XTGOLD          <DIR>       5-20-90    9:22a
XTGOLD    BAT         23    5-20-90    9:23a
WP51            <DIR>       5-20-90   11:23a
HG              <DIR>       5-20-90   11:50a
        21 File(s)   10737664 bytes free
```

Preparing floppy discs

Before you use a floppy disc for the first time, you have to **format** it. This is because the floppy discs you buy can be used with several different types of computer, but have to be set up differently for each one. So before you can use a floppy disc on your PC, you must set the disc up appropriately.

To format a floppy disc, you put the floppy disc in the drive A: (possibly B: if you have two drives and your disc only fits the B: drive). Then (assuming the disc is in drive A:) you type:

c:\>   FORMAT A:

The computer will ask you to insert a disc in drive A: and press Enter when ready.

If the computer displays a message such as "Bad command or file name", it has not been able to find the FORMAT program in your current directory. You will then have to use the CD and DIR commands to find where it is and make sure you are in that directory before typing the FORMAT command. What you are looking for is a file called FORMAT.COM.

Note: Be careful when formatting disc, because is you format a disc which already has already been used to store information, all that information will be lost.

As mentioned in Chapter 1, there are several different kinds of disc drive and you need to make sure you have the correct disc for your drive. Size is one factor (3.5" versus 5.25"); the other is high density versus standard or double density. High density discs are used with AT (80286), 80386 and 80486 machines. Double density discs are generally used with ordinary 8088 or 8086 machines. A machine which can handle high density discs can also use double density discs but machines which use double density discs cannot generally use high density discs.

High density discs can store either 1.4 MB or 1.2 MB whereas double density discs can only store 360 KB or 720 KB.

If you are having problems formatting a disc it is probably because the computer is trying to format a double density disc to 1.4MB or 1.2MB. You should look for the words "high density" on the label of discs which you are formatting with AT or 80386 machines.

Housekeeping in MSDOS
There are a few commands in MSDOS which are very useful for keeping your files in order.

To **rename** a file, you first move to the directory and disc drive where the file is located and then, supposing you wanted to rename MYDATA.DAT to YOURDATA.DAT you would type:

```
c:\>    RENAME MYDATA.DAT YOURDATA.DAT
```

To **copy** a file (of any kind) you follow the following examples.

To copy a file called MYDATA.DAT from whatever directory you happen to be in (say on disc C:) to a disc located in drive A: you type:

```
c:\>    COPY MYDATA.DAT A:
```

To copy all files in the current directory (the directory you are in) which have MYDATA as a prefix and any suffix at all to a disc in drive A:, you type:

```
c:\>    COPY MYDATA.* A:
```

To copy every file in the current directory to a disc in drive A:, you should type:

```
c:\>    COPY *.* A:
```

To copy a file called MYDATA.DAT from a disc in the A: drive to the current directory on drive C: (assuming that you are on drive C:), you should type:

```
c:\>    COPY A:MYDATA.DAT C:
```

If you want to make a copy of a file called EXAMPLE.DAT and you want the copy to be called EXAMPLE2.DAT, you should type:

```
c:\>    COPY EXAMPLE.DAT EXAMPLE2.DAT
```

This assumes that the file to be copied is in the current directory on the C: drive (the current drive), and that you want the new version to be located in the same directory.

The rule is that you use the word COPY followed by two things. The first is what you are copying, and the second is where you are copying it to. If you do not specify a disc drive, MSDOS assumes that you mean the current disc drive. If you do not specify a directory, MSDOS assumes that you mean the current directory. If you want to copy a single file you just use the file name. If you want to copy several files you can use ***** as a **wild card**, either in the prefix part of the file name or in the suffix part or both.

To **delete** a file, you can adapt one of the following examples.

To delete a file called MYDATA.DAT from the current directory, you should type:

`C:\>`   ERASE MYDATA.DAT

To delete a file called MYDATA.DAT from a disc in the A: drive, you would type:

`C:\>`   ERASE A:MYDATA.DAT

To erase all files from a disc in the A: drive, you should type:

`C:\>`   ERASE A:*.*

To erase all files with the prefix MYDATA from the current directory, you would type:

`C:\>`   ERASE MYDATA.*

If you wanted to erase a file called MYDATA.DAT in the \SPSS directory and you did not happen to be in that directory, you would type:

`C:\>`   ERASE \SPSS\MYDATA.DAT

You have probably realized that the rule is that you use the word ERASE followed by a file specification. If the file specification does not include a disc designation it is assumed that you mean the current disc. If the file specification does not include a directory, it is assumed that you mean the current directory. The use of backslashes is required whenever you use a directory specification.

Creating and removing directories

If you want to create a directory, you use the MD command. Suppose that you wanted to create a directory called \DATA on the C: drive. (This could be a convenient location to hold your data files.) You would make sure you were on the C: drive to start with and then type:

```
c:\>    MD \DATA
```

To reassure yourself that this has worked you could type:

```
c:\>    DIR \DATA
```

which will produce a directory listing of the empty DATA directory. Alternatively, you could type:

```
c:\>    DIR \
```

which would produce a listing of the root directory showing the DATA directory in it.

If you want to remove a directory that you do not need any more, you should first use ERASE to get rid of any files in that directory. Then you should make sure that you are not in the directory and type RD followed by the name of the directory. For example, to remove the \DATA directory, you would type:

```
c:\>    RD \DATA
```

A2.2 Creating a data file

MSDOS does not come with a very good editor. Most users employ a separate **word processing** program to create data files. There are lots of these and it would not really be feasible to describe them all. Perhaps the most popular are Wordperfect and Microsoft Word. If you use one of these to create a data file, all you need to remember is that the file has to be an **ASCII** file (sometimes referred to as a **DOS** file, or a **TEXT** file).

Word processors normally store documents in their own

individual format. However they all have a special command to store them as ASCII files if you wish. It is not difficult; you just have to know the right command to use. If you want to use one of these word processors to create your data files, you will have to get instructions from a manual or one of the excellent books that are available.

If you do not have such a word processor, or you do not feel like learning how to use one, I can tell you how to use the MSDOS editor to do the job. A little later on in this Appendix, I will also tell you how to use an editor which comes with SPSSPC+ to create data files.

Using EDLIN to create a data file

The editor that comes with MSDOS is called EDLIN. This editor may be located in the root directory, in a directory called \DOS or in another directory with the rest of the MSDOS operating system files. You should use the DIR command to find out whether a file called **EDLIN.COM** is in one of these directories. Starting with the root directory, search the directories on your hard disc (C:), using the CD and DIR commands until you find which one it is in.

You should then make sure you are in that directory using the CD command.

Suppose that you wish to create a file called **EXAMPLE.DAT** which contains the data given in Appendix 4.

Once you are in the directory containing the file EDLIN.COM, you type the command:

```
C:\>    EDLIN EXAMPLE.DAT
```

You will then see a *. This is the EDLIN prompt. It tells you that EDLIN is waiting for a command.

You wish to insert lines of data into the file, so you press I (standing for insert line), and press Enter. Now you can type in your lines of data one at a time, pressing Enter to mark the end

H

of each line and to move on to the next line. If you make a mistake on the line, you can use the Backspace key to rub out characters back to where you went wrong, and then type in the correct data.

Here is what the screen will look like after you have entered 5 subjects' worth of data:

```
C:\> EDLIN EXAMPLE.DAT
New file
*I
        1:*01 6 4 5 3 6 3 2 3 1 1 32 20 0 1 1 9 9 6 7 13 15 4 1
        2:*02 4 2 4 3 2 2 1 2 1 2 34 23 0 7 9 7 8 7 6 15 20 3 1
        3:*03 5 4 5 3 4 4 2 3 1 1 49 35 0 0 3 3 0 2 3 05 20 3 2
        4:*04 3 3 4 3 2 3 1 2 1 1 29 25 0 1 6 9 6 7 2 13 15 4 3
        5:*05 4 4 3 4 4 4 1 4 1 1 40 21 0 2 9 0 0 4 2 11 20 3 3
```

When you have typed in all the lines of data, or as many as you want to enter for the time being, you press Ctrl-C (hold down the Control key and press C once). This will bring back the * prompt. To finish the session and save the file, you just press E then Enter. This will bring back the system prompt on the screen.

To amend or add to a file called EXAMPLE.DAT, you move to the directory containing EDLIN.COM and then type:

```
C:\>    EDLIN EXAMPLE.DAT
```

The screen will then display a *. You can then get the computer to show you what is in the file by pressing L (standing for "list") then Enter.

This will list the first 23 lines of the file. To list the next 23, you type:

```
*       23,L.
```

The rule is that you can list lines beginning with a particular line number by typing that number followed by a comma followed by L.

Suppose that you want to add further lines of data after the last line, and that the last line is 45 (i.e. there are 45 lines of data already in the file). You would type:

*   47I

This will give you the prompt 46:* at which point you can type your lines of data with each line being terminated with Enter.

The numbering may seem a little odd. It is because **47I** means insert some new lines **before** line 47. You can, if you wish insert new lines anywhere. Just use the number of the line **following** the point where you want to make the insertion.

When you have finished inserting lines, you press **Ctrl-C** to get you back to the EDLIN prompt. If you wish to save the file and exit at this point you press **E** followed by Enter.

If you want to amend a line, you make sure that the cursor is at the EDLIN prompt (*), and then type the number of the line you wish to amend followed by Enter. You can then either type the line in again, or keep pressing the **F1** key (at the top left of the keyboard) to copy characters from the original line until you come to the point which needs changing; then you type in the characters you wish. Pressing Enter will fix the new version of the line. Try this out and you will see what I mean.

To delete a line, you make sure the cursor is at the EDLIN prompt (*), then you type the number of the line you wish to delete followed by **D**. For example, to delete line 23 you type:

*   23D

You should note that whenever you delete a line, the line numbers of all the following lines are reduced by one.

To delete several lines at a time, you specify the line numbers of the first and last lines of the block you want to delete separated by a comma and then **D** followed by Enter, as in:

*   12,24D

which deletes lines 12 to 24 inclusive. Note that what was line 25 now becomes line 12.

You can save your file and exit from EDLIN at any time by making sure that the cursor is at the EDLIN prompt (*) then pressing Crtl-C if you happen to be inserting data, and pressing **E** followed by Enter.

Abandoning the edit

If you want to abandon the EDLIN session without saving any of the changes you have made, you make sure the cursor is at the EDLIN prompt and press **Q** followed by Enter.

Saving files on floppy disc or in different directories

Unless you specify otherwise, the file you create will be located in whatever directory you happened to be in when you started up EDLIN. This is usually not very desirable. It is a simple matter, however, to save your file in a different directory or on a different disc. You just include the disc and/or directory in the file specification.

Remember that when you wanted to start the EDLIN session you typed:

```
c:\>    EDLIN EXAMPLE.DAT
```

Suppose that you had wanted to have the file stored on a disc in the A: drive, you would make sure you have a properly formatted disc in the A: drive and then type:

```
c:\>    EDLIN A:EXAMPLE.DAT
```

Suppose that you want to create the file in a directory called \DATA located on the C: drive, you would type:

```
c:\>    EDLIN C:\DATA\EXAMPLE.DAT
```

You must obviously have created such a directory some time before.

The same rule applies if you want to amend an existing file

which is not in the current directory. For example, to amend a file called EXAMPLE.DAT located on a disc in the A: drive, you type:

```
c:\>   EDLIN A:EXAMPLE.DAT
```

A2.3 A recap on MSDOS and EDLIN

You need to know about MSDOS to be able to use SPSS or MINITAB and to be able to create and keep track of your data files.

To create a data file you can move to the directory where a file called EDLIN.COM is located. You can then use EDLIN to type in your data and save it in a file. Once you have done this you can amend the data file, also using EDLIN.

The thing to remember about MSDOS is that you need to keep track of which disc and directory is **current** (the one that you are in at the moment), and on which disc and in what directory the files that you wish to use are located.

A2.4 Beginning, running and ending an SPSSPC+ session.

To start an SPSSPC+ session, you go into the SPSS directory (by typing CD \SPSS) and type:

```
c:\>   SPSSPC
```

After a few moments' delay you will see the SPSS logo and then moments later, the SPSS **menu system**. Here is what the screen will look like:

```
═══════ MAIN MENU ═══════        ─────────── orientation ───────────
orientation                      The "orientation" section provides a brief
read or write data               explanation of how the SPSS/PC+ Menu and Help
modify data or files             system works.  If you have not used the
graph data                       Menu and Help system before, you may want to
analyze data                     read through the screens in the orientation.
session control & info           To do so, press ◄┘ (Enter).
run DOS or other pgms
─extended menus───               Part A of the SPSS/PC+ V3.0 update manual contains
─SPSS/PC+ options─               a list of modifications and new features in V3.0.
FINISH                           Part A of the SPSS/PC+ V2.0 manual contains a more
                                 complete introduction to the Menu and Help system.
                                 ──── F1=Help   Alt-E=Edit   Alt-M=Menus on/off ────
```

```
                                            ═Ins══════════Std Menus═ 01
                                              scratch.pad
```

J

Almost no-one I know uses the menu system because it is very cumbersome. I will tell you how to turn the menu system off and use SPSSPC+ just like you would use SPSS-X. I will then tell you how to take advantage of SPSSPC+'s in-built editor called REVIEW to enter commands and data, and to view results. Finally, I will show you how to turn the menu system back on again so that you can use its **help facilities**.

Turning the menu system off

When you first go into SPSSPC+, this is what you do to turn the menu system off:

Press **Alt-M** (hold down the Alt key and press M once).

Keeping the menu system off and staying out of Review

To avoid going back into the menu each time you execute a command, and to use SPSSPC+ as you would SPSS-X, you should now type:

```
SET /RUNREVIEW MANUAL /AUTOMENU OFF.
```

Press Enter at the end of the line.

Then, use the up cursor key to move the cursor back so that it is on the line you have just typed, press the **F10** key; then press Enter. You will then see the SPSS prompt SPSS/PC: at the bottom of the screen with the flashing cursor next to it.

You are now ready to type in commands just as if you were using SPSS-X. Read the section on using SPSS-X in Appendix 1.

The main part of this book explains how to use these commands to get the statistical analyses you want.

When you have finished your analysis for the time being, you type:

*SPSS/PC:*STOP.

This will exit from SPSSPC+ and get you back to the system prompt.

You now know enough to be able to use this book to run statistical analyses using SPSSPC+. The next section explains about an editor which comes with SPSSPC+ which can save you time and effort. You do not have to read about it if you already feel overloaded. Perhaps you could come back to it later.

Note: When SPSSPC+ displays results on the screen, it does so one screenful at a time. It then beeps and prints

MORE?

at the top right of the screen. You should press the Enter key when you are ready for the next screenful.

A2.5 The Review editor

Review is a text editor which allows you to:

- type in, amend and execute commands to SPSSPC+

- save sets of commands so that you can use them again

- view the results of any statistical analyses you have carried out in the current session

- save these results as a file which you can then go back to and look at again or incorporate into a document created by a word processing program

- type in and save data using an editor which is more convenient than EDLIN

Getting into the Review editor

Suppose that you have just gone into SPSSPC+. You have the menu system on the screen. You press **Alt-M** to get rid of this. **You are now in the Review editor.**

You will see that the screen is divided into an upper and a lower portion. The upper portion is called the **Results Window**. The lower portion is called the **Command Window**. The upper portion displays the results of any analyses you undertake and the lower portion is for you to type commands in.

The first command you should type having entered Review

The first command you should type in when you go into the Review editor is this:

SET AUTOMENU OFF.

You then execute this command by making sure the cursor is on this line (it does not matter where) and pressing **F10** followed by Enter. If you do not execute this command, every time you get SPSSPC+ to execute a command, it will put you back into the menu system rather than the Review editor. You would then have to press **Alt-M** each time to get you into Review. This is not a major inconvenience but becomes irritating after a while.

Using the review editor to execute commands

To use Review to give commands to SPSSPC+, this is what you do:

a.   Type in one or more lines of text corresponding to commands for SPSSPC+.

b.   Move the cursor up to the **first** of these lines.

c.   Press **F10** followed by Enter to execute these commands.

d.   View the results as they come on the screen.

e.   You will then be returned to the Review editor at which point you can type in more commands or modify the commands you typed in before and perform further analyses.

Note that you can type in and execute one command at a time if you wish, or you can type in several commands and execute them all at once.

To exit from SPSSPC+ using the Review editor
To exit from SPSSPC+, while in the Review editor you should type the command:

STOP.

(You do not need to press the Enter key)

Then with the cursor still on that line, press **F10** followed by Enter.

Amending commands using Review
To amend one or more commands that you have already typed in using Review, you just move the cursor to the part which you want to amend and use the Backspace key to delete unwanted text; then add the new text in its place.

Executing a block of commands using Review
To execute a particular series of lines, anywhere in the command window (e.g. ones you have just amended) you move the cursor to the **first** line in the set of lines (**block**) that you want to execute and press **F7** followed by Enter. You then move the cursor to the **last** line in the block you want to execute and press **F7** again. This marks the block (or **area**) out. You then press **F10**. This brings up a menu at the bottom of the screen. One of the options in the menu is "Run marked area". You press the **right-cursor key** once so that this option is highlighted. Then you press Enter.

Viewing previous results using Review

To examine results of analyses carried out previously in the session, you press **F2** followed by Enter. This switches you to the Results Window. You can then use the cursor keys to move around. If you move the cursor to the top of the window and carry on pressing the up cursor key, the window will scroll to reveal text above that already displayed. A similar principle operates for seeing material that is out of sight because it comes **after** the text in the Results Window.

To switch back to the Command Window again, you press **F2** followed by Enter.

Using Review to create data files and command files.

It is possible to use the Review editor to create files containing data or SPSS commands. What you do is to type in the text using the Enter key at the end of each line and the Backspace key to delete text. The cursor keys move you around the text. When you have typed in the text or data you want, you move the cursor to the **first** of the lines you want to save in a file and press **F7** followed by Enter. Then you move the cursor to the **last** line and press **F7** again (but not Enter). This marks a block or area.

You then press **F9**. This brings up a menu at the bottom of the screen. One of the options in the menu is "Write marked area". You press the right-cursor key once to highlight this option and press Enter. You are then prompted at the bottom of the screen for Name for file. You should type in the name you wish to give the file (e.g. EXAMPLE.RUN), then press Enter.

This will save the file in the current directory. If you want to save the file to a disc in drive A:, you should put A: in front of the file name (e.g. A: EXAMPLE.RUN). If you wish to save the file in a directory called \DATA (assuming there is such a directory on your hard disc), you put the directory name in the file specification (e.g. \DATA\EXAMPLE.RUN).

Note: You can use this to create data files instead of a text editor. Just type in data instead of commands, and save it as though you were saving commands.

You can use this to create files containing your results by using **F2** to switch to the Results Window, marking out a block in that window as described above and then saving it using **F9**.

Executing stored commands in SPSSPC+

If you want to execute a set of commands which you have previously saved on disc in a file, you get into Review and then type the command:

```
INCLUDE 'XXXXX.XXX'.
```

where XXXXX.XXX is the name of the file you saved the commands in. The single quotes must be typed in, as must the full stop. Then put the cursor on this line and press F10 followed by Enter.

Note that this assumes that the file is in the current directory. If you have put the file on a disc in the A: drive you would type:

```
INCLUDE 'A:XXXXX.XXX'.
```

Exactly the same principles apply when using files in SPSSPC+ as apply in MSDOS. Unless you specify a directory, SPSSPC+ will assume that you are dealing with the current directory. Unless you specify a disc drive, it is assumed that you mean the current disc drive.

If you wanted to execute commands saved in a file called EXAMPLE.RUN in a directory called \DATA, you would execute the command:

```
INCLUDE '\DATA\EXAMPLE.RUN'.
```

Remember that to execute a command you must type it in then make sure that the cursor is on that line and press **F10** followed by Enter.

A2.6 Running MINITAB on PCs

To run MINITAB on your PC, you use CD to move to the directory containing the file called MINITAB.COM (usually the directory will be called \MINITAB). You then simply type:

```
c:\>    MINITAB
```

and press Enter.

This will bring up the MINITAB prompt, which is:

```
MTB>
```

To use MINITAB on the PC, you type the commands in exactly as you would with the mainframe version. (See the relevant section in Appendix 1.)

To exit from MINITAB, you type:

```
MTB>    STOP
```

and press Enter. This gets you back to the system prompt.

Executing stored commands in MINITAB

If you have a set of MINITAB commands that you may want to use several times, perhaps on different data files, then you can save yourself a lot of typing by storing the commands in a file and then issuing a special command to MINITAB to execute the commands in that file.

You first create the file with the commands in. To do this, you use EDLIN, as described in this appendix. This is exactly the same as creating a data file, but instead of putting numbers in it, you put MINITAB commands. Let us suppose that you have created a file called EXAMPLE2.RUN with the following lines in it:

```
READ 'EXAMPLE.DAT' C1-C24
CODE (9) '*' C2-C11
CODE (99) '*' C12 C13 C22
DESCR C2 C4 C6 C8
TABLE C10;
STATS C2 C4 C6 C8.
```

Then you finish the EDLIN session (press Ctrl-C followed by E then Enter) and go into MINITAB. Once you are in MINITAB, to execute the commands in EXAMPLE2.RUN you would type:

MTB>   EXECUTE 'EXAMPLE2.RUN'

Recap

To use SPSSPC+ or the PC version of MINITAB, you first need to create a file containing the data you want to analyze. You can do this using a word processing program, or using EDLIN as described in this appendix. Then you move to the directory containing SPSSPC+ or MINITAB (type CD \SPSS or CD \MINITAB) and type SPSSPC or MINITAB to enter one of these programs.

SPSSPC+ can be run in two different ways (not counting use of the menu system).

•   You can type in the commands as though it were SPSS-X.

•   You can use the Review editor to construct commands which you then execute. The Review editor can also be used to create data files, files containing the results of analyses or files containing SPSSPC+ commands.

MINITAB is used in the same way as the mainframe version by typing commands which are then executed directly (see Appendix 1).

You should try out what you can now. Do not be afraid to mess things up. You will only learn by doing and by continually referring back to this appendix when you get stuck. Hopefully, you will have someone to help you out, but if not, you should be able to figure it out as long as you persevere.

Using on-line help facilities

SPSSPC+ and MINITAB have very good help facilities which you can use if you are not sure what to do, or if you want to learn more about these packages than has been covered in this book.

Help with SPSSPC+

You obtain help from SPSSPC+ by moving through the menu system. You may remember that I suggested that you turn the menu system off as soon as you began a session of SPSSPC+ because it is a rather cumbersome way of issuing commands. However, it is the only way that you can obtain help from SPSSPC+.

When you are in the Review editor (with the upper half of the screen as the results window and the lower half as the command window) you can press Alt-M (hold down the Alt key and press M once) to turn the menu system on. Remember that you also pressed Alt-M to turn the menu system off. Alt-M is a toggle key which turns the menu system on and off.

With the menu system on, you can use the cursor keys to gain help on all aspects of the workings of SPSSPC+.

You use the up or down cursor keys to move between different items in the current menu (on the left hand side of the screen). Whatever item you happen to be on will have a help message displayed on the right hand side of the upper part of the screen.

You can use the right cursor key to move to a new submenu corresponding to the item that the cursor is currently on.

If you want to move back again to the higher level menu, you press the left cursor key.

You can turn the menu system off at any time by pressing Alt-M.

Try pressing the down cursor key and up cursor key. You will see that different lines in the top left hand part of the screen will be highlighted. Move the cursor so that the "analyze data" option is highlighted. Then press the right cursor key. This will produce the following display.

```
━━━━━ analyze data ━━━━━        ┌───── descriptive statistics ─────
descriptive statistics          Select "descriptive statistics" for:
reports and tables              FREQUENCIES, which displays frequency
correlation & regression        tables, statistics, bar charts, and
comparing group means           histograms.
classification & clustering     DESCRIPTIVES, which displays descriptive
time series                     statistics that do not require a frequency
other                           table, and optionally creates Z-scores.
                                CROSSTABS, which displays bivariate
                                distributions in the form of cross-
                                tabulations, with measures of association.
                                MEANS, which displays means for subgroups.
                                └─ Press Alt or Alt-- to scroll window ──▾

━━━━━━━━━━━━━━━━━━━━━━━━━━━━━━━━━━━━━━━Ins━━━━━━━━Std Menus▪ 01
                                      scratch.pad
```

Now move the cursor (pressing the up or down cursor key) so that the item "descriptive statistics" is highlighted. Then press the right cursor key again to produce the following display.

```
┏━━━ DESCRIPTIVES ━━━       ┌─────── -examples- ───────
┃ -examples-                │ 1. simple example:
┃ !/VARIABLES               │ DESCRIPTIVES /VARIABLES score1 score2 score3.
┃  /OPTIONS                 │
┃  /STATISTICS              │ 2. options and statistics:
┃                           │ DESCRIPTIVES /VARIABLES age var1 to var5 income
┃                           │ /OPTIONS 3 5 /STATISTICS ALL.
┃                           │
┃                           │
┃                           │
┗━━ ! = required ━━┛        └ F1=Help  Esc=Cancel  Alt-E=Edit  Alt-M=Menus on/off ┘


DESCRIPTIVES━━━━━━━━━━━━━━━━━━━━━━━━━━━━Ins━━━━━━━━Std Menus▪ 01
                                        scratch.pad
```

This display now shows how to use the DESCRIPTIVES command described in Chapter 5 of this book. You may note that in the examples used in this book, I use abbreviated forms of the command (e.g. DESCR).

Now if you want to return to the main menu you can press the left cursor key until you get there.

You should try out this help system until you get the hang of it.

Help with MINITAB on the PC

You obtain help with the PC version of MINITAB in exactly the same way as with the mainframe version. Please see Appendix 1 for details.

Appendix 3

Example SPSS and MINITAB sessions

This appendix contains sample SPSS and MINITAB sessions including many of the commands used as examples in this book. There are four sessions, one each for: 1) SPSS-X, 2) SPSSPC+, 3) MINITAB on mainframes, and 4) MINITAB on PCs.

You should try running these sessions for yourself. If you do not feel like typing in the whole session, just run some of the commands.

A3.1 A session including many of the commands for SPSS-X used in this book

To run this session, you should type the following just once:

(Press Enter and type in user name and then password in response to the prompts)

```
$     EDIT EXAMPLE.DAT
*     C
      01 6 4 5 3 6 3 2 3 1 1 32 20 0 1 1 9 9 6 7 13 15 4 1
      02 4 2 4 3 2 2 1 2 1 2 34 23 0 7 9 7 8 7 6 15 20 3 1
      03 5 4 5 3 4 4 2 3 1 1 49 35 0 0 3 3 0 2 3 05 20 3 2
```

(and all the remaining data in Appendix 4)
(Press Ctrl-Z - hold down the Ctrl key and press Z)

```
*     EXIT

$     SPSSX /OUTPUT=RESULTS.RES

SPSS-X>  DATA LIST FILE=EXAMPLE.DAT FREE / SUBNO
CONT>    CRAV1 DIFF1 CRAV2 DIFF2 CRAV3 DIFF3 CRAV4
CONT>    DIFF4 SEX COND AGE CO PSY HAND INDUL SED
```

```
CONT>    STIM AUTO ADD DEPEND CIGSPD MOTIV TROUB.

SPSS-X> MISSING VALUES CRAV1 TO DIFF4 SEX (9) AGE CO
CONT>    CIGSPD (99).

SPSS-X> LIST VAR=SUBNO.

SPSS-X> SAVE OUTFILE=EXAMPLE.SYS.

SPSS-X> STOP.
```

Having the done the above once, you can type in the first two and then any or all of the other commands listed below in subsequent sessions. However, it is almost certain that you will have made at least one mistake in the above and will have to edit the data file and try reading it into SPSS several times before it finally works.

```
$       SPSS /OUTPUT=RESULTS.RES

SPSS-X> GET FILE=EXAMPLE.SYS.

SPSS-X> DESCR VAR=CRAV1 CRAV2 CRAV3 CRAV4.

SPSS-X> MEANS CRAV1 CRAV2 CRAV3 CRAV4 BY SEX BY
CONT>    COND.

SPSS-X> FREQ VAR=CRAV1 CRAV2 CRAV3 CRAV4
CONT>    /STAT=MEDIAN.

SPSS-X> FREQ VAR=CRAV1 TO DIFF4.

SPSS-X> FREQ VAR=SEX COND /FORMAT=NOTABLE /HIST.

SPSS-X> CROSS SEX BY COND /CELLS=ROW COLUMN
CONT>    /STAT=CHISQ.

SPSS-X> CORR CRAV1 TO DIFF4 / PRINT = TWOTAIL /
CONT>    MISSING = PAIRWISE.

SPSS-X> NONPAR CORR CRAV1 TO DIFF4 / PRINT = TWOTAIL
CONT>    / MISSING = PAIRWISE.

SPSS-X> PLOT PLOT=CIGSPD WITH DEPEND.

SPSS-X> T-TEST GROUPS = SEX(1,2) / VAR = DEPEND.
```

```
SPSS-X> NPAR TESTS M-W=CRAV1 CRAV2 CRAV3 CRAV4 BY SEX(1,2).

SPSS-X> NPAR TESTS K-W=CRAV1 BY COND(1,4).

SPSS-X> ANOVA CRAV1 BY COND(1,4) SEX(1,2).

SPSS-X> ONEWAY CRAV1 BY COND(1,4) /RANGES=
CONT>    SCHEFFE(.05).

SPSS-X> T-TEST PAIRS=CRAV1 CRAV2.

SPSS-X> NPAR TESTS WILCOXON=CRAV1 WITH CRAV2.

SPSS-X> MANOVA CRAV1 CRAV2 CRAV3 CRAV4 /
CONT>    WSFACTORS=TIME(4).

SPSS-X> NPAR TESTS FRIEDMAN=CRAV1 CRAV2 CRAV3
CONT>    CRAV4.

SPSS-X> MANOVA CRAV1 CRAV2 CRAV3 CRAV4 /
CONT>    WSFACTORS = TIME(4) / CONTRAST(TIME) =
CONT>    SPECIAL=(1 1 1 1 -3 1 1 1 0 -2 1 1 0 0 -1 1) /
CONT>    PRINT = SIGNIF(UNIV).

SPSS-X> MANOVA CRAV1 CRAV2 CRAV3 CRAV4 DIFF1 DIFF2
CONT>    DIFF3 DIFF4 BY COND(1,4) SEX(1,2)/WSFAC=
CONT>    SCORETYP(2) TIME(4).

SPSS-X> REGRESS VAR=PSY HAND INDUL SED STIM AUTO
CONT>    ADD CRAV1 / DEP=CRAV1 / METHOD=ENTER.

SPSS-X> FACTOR VAR=PSY TO ADD / EXTR=ML /
CONT>    ROTAT=VARIMAX.

SPSS-X> CLUSTER CRAV1 CRAV2 CRAV3 CRAV4 /
CONT>    PLOT=DEND.

SPSS-X> DISCRIM GROUPS = COND(1,4) / VAR = CRAV1 CRAV2
CONT>    CRAV3 CRAV4 / METHOD = DIRECT / STAT=TABLE.

SPSS-X> STOP.
```

If, after a session of this kind, you want to view the results contained in RESULTS.RES, you type:

```
$      EDIT RESULTS.RES
*      C
```

(Then you use the cursor keys to move around the results file to view the parts of interest to you)

```
        Ctrl-Z (hold down Ctrl and press Z once)
*       QUIT
```

If you want to print the results contained in RESULTS.RES, you type:

```
$       PRINT RESULTS.RES
```

When you have finished the session, you type:

```
$       LOGOUT
```

A3.2 A session including many of the commands for SPSSPC+ used in this book

To run this session, you should type the following.

```
c:\>    CD \SPSS
c:\>    SPSS
```

(This will display the SPSSPC+ menu system)

(Press Alt-M - hold down the Alt key and press M once)

(Type in the following data)
```
01 6 4 5 3 6 3 2 3 1 1 32 20 0 1 1 9 9 6 7 13 15 4 1
02 4 2 4 3 2 2 1 2 1 2 34 23 0 7 9 7 8 7 6 15 20 3 1
03 5 4 5 3 4 4 2 3 1 1 49 35 0 0 3 3 0 2 3 05 20 3 2
```
(and all the remaining data in Appendix 4)

(Use the up cursor key to move the flashing cursor so that it is somewhere on the **first** line of the data)

(Press F7)
(Press Enter)

(Use the down cursor key to move the flashing cursor to the **last** line of the data)

(Press F7)
(Press F9)
(Press the right cursor key once so that the words "Write marked area" are highlighted)
(Press Enter)
(Make sure that you have a formatted floppy disc in drive A: on your computer)
(Type A:EXAMPLE.DAT)
(Press Enter)

(Type the following commands pressing Enter to end each line)

```
DATA LIST FILE='A:EXAMPLE.DAT' FREE / SUBNO CRAV1
DIFF1 CRAV2 DIFF2 CRAV3 DIFF3 CRAV4 DIFF4 SEX COND AGE
CO PSY HAND INDUL SED STIM AUTO ADD DEPEND CIGSPD
MOTIV TROUB.
MISSING VALUES CRAV1 TO DIFF4 SEX (9) AGE CO CIGSPD
(99).
LIST VAR=SUBNO.
```

(When you have typed in all these lines, move the cursor so that it is somewhere on the line beginning DATA LIST)
(Press F10 then Enter.)

(You will see the DATA LIST command being executed, followed by the LIST command.)

If all is well, the subject numbers 1 to 56 will appear on the screen.

More likely, you will get an error message or a warning. This means that either the data in EXAMPLE.DAT or the DATA LIST command have something wrong with them.

If it seems that the data file might have errors in it, you do not have to type the data all in again. Do the following:

(Press F3)
(Press the right cursor key once to highlight the words "Insert file")
(Type A:EXAMPLE.DAT and press Enter)

(You will see the lines of data which you typed in appear on the screen.)

(Move the cursor around using the cursor keys until you find the part which needs correcting and then use the Backspace key at the top right of the keyboard to delete the unwanted numbers, then type in the correct numbers.)

(When you have made the necessary corrections, use the up cursor key to move the flashing cursor so that it is somewhere on the first line of the data.)
(Press F7)
(Press Enter)

(Use the down cursor key to move the cursor to the last line of data.)
(Press F7)
(Press F9)
(Press the right cursor key once until the words "Write marked area" are highlighted at the bottom of the screen.)
(Make sure you have a properly formatted floppy disc in the A: drive of the computer.)
(Type A:EXAMPLE.DAT and press Enter.)

Now type in the sequence of commands beginning with DATA LIST again and execute them by placing the cursor on the line beginning DATA LIST, and pressing F10 followed by Enter.

Repeat this exercise until there are no warning or error messages.

Now type:

SAVE OUTFILE='A:EXAMPLE.SYS'.

(Press Enter)
(Press the up cursor key to move the cursor back to this line)
(Press F10 followed by Enter)

This should save a system file on your disc in drive A:

Now type:

```
STOP.
```

(Press Enter)
(Press the up cursor key once so that the cursor in on the line with STOP in it)
(Press F10 and Enter)

This will end the SPSSPC+ session and bring back the system prompt:

```
c:\>
```

Having done the above once, you can begin any subsequent sessions using EXAMPLE.SYS as follows - you do not need to type the data in again and you do not need to use the DATA LIST command.

```
c:\>    CD \SPSS
c:\>    SPSS
```

(Press Alt-M)

Type:

```
SET AUTOMENU OFF.
SET RUNREVIEW MANUAL.
```

(Press Enter after each line)
(Press the up cursor key twice so that the cursor is on the line containing SET AUTOMENU OFF.)
(Press F10 followed by Enter)

This brings up the SPSSPC+ prompt.

Then type:

```
SPSS/PC:GET FILE='A:EXAMPLE.SYS'.
```

Now you can type any or all of the following commands:

```
SPSS/PC:DESCR VAR=CRAV1 CRAV2 CRAV3 CRAV4.
```

```
SPSS/PC:MEANS CRAV1 CRAV2 CRAV3 CRAV4 BY SEX BY
CONT>   COND.

SPSS/PC:FREQ VAR=CRAV1 CRAV2 CRAV3 CRAV4
CONT>   /STAT=MEDIAN.

SPSS/PC:FREQ VAR=CRAV1 TO DIFF4.

SPSS/PC:FREQ VAR=SEX COND /FORMAT=NOTABLE /HIST.

SPSS/PC:CROSS SEX BY COND / OPT=3 4 /STAT=1

SPSS/PC:CORR CRAV1 TO DIFF4 / OPT=2 3 5.

SPSS/PC:CROSS DEPEND BY CIGSPD /STAT=6.

SPSS/PC:PLOT PLOT=CIGSPD WITH DEPEND.

SPSS/PC:T-TEST GROUPS = SEX(1,2) / VAR = DEPEND.

SPSS/PC:NPAR TESTS M-W=CRAV1 CRAV2 CRAV3 CRAV4 BY SEX(1,2).

SPSS/PC:NPAR TESTS K-W=CRAV1 BY COND(1,4).

SPSS/PC:ANOVA CRAV1 BY COND(1,4) SEX(1,2).

SPSS/PC:ONEWAY CRAV1 BY COND(1,4) /RANGES=
CONT>   SCHEFFE(.05).

SPSS/PC:T-TEST PAIRS=CRAV1 CRAV2.

SPSS/PC:NPAR TESTS WILCOXON=CRAV1 WITH CRAV2.

SPSS/PC:MANOVA CRAV1 CRAV2 CRAV3 CRAV4 /
CONT>   WSFACTORS=TIME(4).

SPSS/PC:NPAR TESTS FRIEDMAN=CRAV1 CRAV2 CRAV3
CONT>   CRAV4.

SPSS/PC:MANOVA CRAV1 CRAV2 CRAV3 CRAV4 /
CONT>   WSFACTORS = TIME(4) / CONTRAST(TIME) =
CONT>   SPECIAL (1 1 1 1 -3 1 1 1 0 -2 1 1 0 0 -1 1) /
CONT>   PRINT = SIGNIF(UNIV).

SPSS/PC:MANOVA CRAV1 CRAV2 CRAV3 CRAV4 DIFF1 DIFF2
CONT>   DIFF3 DIFF4 BY COND(1,4) SEX(1,2)/WSFAC=
CONT>   SCORETYP(2) TIME(4).

SPSS/PC:REGRESS VAR=PSY HAND INDUL SED STIM AUTO
CONT>   ADD CRAV1 / DEP=CRAV1 / METHOD=ENTER.
```

```
SPSS/PC:FACTOR VAR=PSY TO ADD / EXTR=ML /
CONT>   ROTAT=VARIMAX.

SPSS/PC:CLUSTER CRAV1 CRAV2 CRAV3 CRAV4 /
CONT>   PLOT=DEND.

SPSS/PC:DISCRIM GROUPS = COND(1,4) / VAR = CRAV1 CRAV2
CONT>   CRAV3 CRAV4 / METHOD = DIRECT / STAT=13.

SPSS/PC:STOP.
```

A3.3 A session including many of the commands used in this book for MINITAB on mainframes

To run this session, you should create the file EXAMPLE.DAT as follows.

(Press Enter and type in user name and then password in responde to the prompts)

```
$       EDIT EXAMPLE.DAT
*       C
        01 6 4 5 3 6 3 2 3 1 1 32 20 0 1 1 9 9 6 7 13 15 4 1
        02 4 2 4 3 2 2 1 2 1 2 34 23 0 7 9 7 8 7 6 15 20 3 1
        03 5 4 5 3 4 4 2 3 1 1 49 35 0 0 3 3 0 2 3 05 20 3 2
        (and all the remaining data in Appendix 4)
        (Press Ctrl-Z - hold down the Ctrl key and press Z)
*       EXIT
```

(Now you can go into MINITAB)

```
$       MINITAB


MTB>    READ 'EXAMPLE.DAT' C1-C24

MTB>    CODE (9) '*' C2-C11 C2-C11

MTB>    CODE (99) '*' C12-C13 C22 C12 C13 C22

MTB>    SAVE 'EXAMPLE.MTB'

MTB>    PRINT C1
```

```
MTB>    STOP
```

(If all is well, you should see the subject numbers 1 to 56 appear on the screen. More likely, you will get an error message or warning. In that case, there is probably something wrong with your data file. You should go back to the EDIT command to find the error and correct it.)

Once the above commands have been successfully carried out once, for all subsequent sessions you type:

```
$       MINITAB
MTB>    RETR 'EXAMPLE.MTB'
```

and then any or all of the following commands.

```
MTB>    LET C25=C2+C3

MTB>    RSUM C14-C20 C28

MTB>    RSD C14-C20 C29

MTB>    DESCR C2 C4 C6 C8

MTB>    TABLES C10;
SUBC>   STATS C2 C4 C6 C8.

MTB>    HIST C10 C11

MTB>    TABLE C23 BY C24;
SUBC>   COLPERCENTS;
SUBC>   CHISQ.

MTB>    CORR C2-C9

MTB>    PLOT C21 C22

MTB>    TWOT C2 C10

MTB>    KRUS C2 C10

MTB>    ONEWAY C2 C11

MTB>    KRUS C2 C11

MTB>    ANOVA C2=C10 C11 C10*C11
```

```
MTB>    REGRESS C2 7 C14-C20

MTB>    STEPWISE C2 C14-C20

MTB>    DISCRIM C11 C2 C4 C6 C8

MTB>    STOP

$       LOGOUT
```

A3.4 A session including most of the commands used in this book for MINITAB on PCs

To run this session, you should create the file EXAMPLE.DAT as follows.

(Make sure you have a formatted floppy disc in the A: drive of your computer for the whole of this session.)

```
c:\>    EDLIN A:EXAMPLE.DAT
*       I

        01 6 4 5 3 6 3 2 3 1 1 32 20 0 1 1 9 9 6 7 13 15 4 1
        02 4 2 4 3 2 2 1 2 1 2 34 23 0 7 9 7 8 7 6 15 20 3 1
        03 5 4 5 3 4 4 2 3 1 1 49 35 0 0 3 3 0 2 3 05 20 3 2
```
(Type in all the remaining data from Appendix 4)

(Press Ctrl-C - hold down the Ctrl key and press C once)

```
*       EXIT

c:\>    CD \MINITAB
c:\>    MINITAB

MTB>    READ 'A:EXAMPLE.DAT' C1-C24

MTB>    CODE (9) '*' C2-C11 C2-C11

MTB>    CODE (99) '*' C12 C13 C22 C12 C13 C22

MTB>    SAVE 'A:EXAMPLE.MTB'

MTB>    PRINT C1

MTB>    STOP
```

(If all is well, you should see the subject numbers 1 to 56 appear on the screen. More likely, you will get an error message or warning. In that case, there is probably something wrong with your data file. You should go back to the EDLIN command to find the error and correct it.)

After the above commands have been successfully carried out once, for all subsequent sessions you type:

```
C:\>    MINITAB
MTB>    RETR 'A:EXAMPLE.MTB'
```

and then any or all of the following commands:

```
MTB>    LET C25=C2+C3

MTB>    RSUM C14-C20 C28

MTB>    RSD C14-C20 C29

MTB>    DESCR C2 C4 C6 C8

MTB>    TABLES C10;
SUBC>   STATS C2 C4 C6 C8.

MTB>    HIST C10 C11

MTB>    TABLE C23 BY C24;
SUBC>   COLPERCENTS;
SUBC>   CHISQ.

MTB>    CORR C2-C9

MTB>    PLOT C21 C22

MTB>    TWOT C2 C10

MTB>    KRUS C2 C10

MTB>    ONEWAY C2 C11

MTB>    KRUS C2 C11

MTB>    ANOVA C2=C10 C11 C10*C11
```

MTB>   REGRESS C2 7 C14—C20

MTB>   STEPWISE C2 C14—C20

MTB>   DISCRIM C11 C2 C4 C6 C8

MTB>   STOP

Appendix 4

EXAMPLE.DAT, an example data file

This appendix gives data which can be stored in a file called EXAMPLE.DAT to illustrate the use of commands in this book. You should create this data file with the help of Appendix 1 or 2 if you are using a VAX with VMS or PC with MSDOS. Appendix 3 gives complete examples of how to create this file. If you are using a different kind of computer you will have to take advice on how to create the data file.

Only the numbers should be typed in. You should set out the data file exactly as is shown here. Each line should begin at the left hand-margin, and there should be one space between each variable.

```
01 6 4 5 3 6 3 2 3 1 1 32 20 0 1 1 9 9 6 7 13 15 4 1
02 4 2 4 3 2 2 1 2 1 2 34 23 0 7 9 7 8 7 6 15 20 3 1
03 5 4 5 3 4 4 2 3 1 1 49 35 0 0 3 3 0 2 3 05 20 3 2
04 3 3 4 3 2 3 1 2 1 1 29 25 0 1 6 9 6 7 2 13 15 4 3
05 4 4 3 4 4 4 1 4 1 1 40 21 0 2 9 0 0 4 2 11 20 3 3
06 3 3 3 5 2 3 1 2 2 2 44 30 0 2 6 8 4 2 2 07 35 4 1
07 3 3 2 3 3 3 2 2 2 2 46 32 1 1 3 6 6 9 1 18 40 6 2
08 3 3 2 3 2 3 1 3 1 1 99 37 2 4 1 6 8 9 3 18 40 6 2
09 3 2 3 2 2 2 2 1 2 41 15 1 4 5 9 6 7 5 15 25 4 2
10 3 2 3 2 2 2 1 3 1 2 42 19 1 8 5 9 4 9 9 18 30 4 3
11 3 3 3 3 2 3 2 2 1 2 45 29 0 8 4 8 2 2 8  4 20 7 2
12 4 3 3 1 4 3 1 2 1 2 46 39 0 6 4 8 9 6 2 14 40 5 1
13 3 2 2 2 2 2 3 2 2 2 27 30 0 0 2 6 3 5 4 11 24 4 2
14 3 2 2 2 1 2 1 3 1 2 26 31 0 1 4 8 4 7 5 15 35 4 2
15 2 4 3 4 2 4 2 3 1 3 45 18 3 2 3 6 4 0 11 20 5 4
16 2 3 4 3 2 3 1 4 1 3 45 23 0 7 3 9 7 7 4 14 25 4 1
17 4 1 3 1 2 1 1 1 2 2 26 29 0 2 5 8 4 6 7 11 35 4 1
18 1 1 1 1 1 1 2 1 2 3 35 26 5 7 6 9 2 8 4 15 30 4 1
19 2 3 1 3 1 3 2 3 1 4 36 21 3 6 5 9 5 7 4 13 30 4 2
20 1 3 1 3 1 2 1 4 1 3 23 25 3 7 6 9 9 6 3 14 20 5 3
21 2 3 2 2 1 2 1 2 2 3 26 19 2 4 4 9 5 7 4 13 20 4 2
22 2 2 2 2 2 2 2 2 2 4 37 27 1 6 7 7 8 7 1 16 24 5 3
23 2 1 2 1 2 1 2 2 2 4 21 21 0 1 8 8 6 4 1  9 20 4 1
24 1 3 1 3 1 3 1 2 1 4 33 12 3 5 5 5 1 2 1  7  8 2 3
25 2 1 1 1 2 1 3 1 1 4 25 23 0 2 5 9 5 8 2 16 25 4 2
26 2 3 1 3 1 3 2 2 1 4 45 45 0 0 6 9 3 9 4 17 30 4 2
```

```
27 1 1 2 2 1 1 2 1 2 4 52 32 6 9 3 9 5 7 1 16 55 2 2
28 6 4 5 4 4 4 2 3 2 1 48 23 0 1 8 7 5 2 8  6 99 7 2
29 2 3 1 3 2 3 2 2 2 4 32 34 0 0 3 0 2 8 3 17 40 6 2
30 6 5 4 4 3 5 1 4 2 1 29 27 3 1 4 9 5 7 5 16 40 4 1
31 6 6 5 3 4 6 2 5 2 1 50 16 2 0 4 6 7 7 9 11 10 7 3
32 3 2 1 2 3 2 3 2 2 4 37 23 0 7 6 4 0 8 3 16 35 6 2
33 6 3 4 3 3 3 2 2 2 1 56 19 5 0 4 7 6 2 6  8 25 4 1
34 4 2 3 2 3 2 1 3 2 2 27 16 0 8 5 9 4 6 2 13 20 4 1
35 5 5 4 5 3 5 1 4 2 1 69 16 0 0 4 6 0 4 3  6 12 4 1
36 4 2 4 2 4 2 1 2 2 2 46 30 4 6 3 9 0 5 2 11 20 4 1
37 2 4 1 4 2 4 2 3 1 4 38 12 0 3 5 8 2 3 0  7  8 4 2
38 2 2 2 2 2 2 2 2 2 4 39 23 4 3 7 9 1 7 0 14 20 4 1
39 2 3 2 3 1 3 2 2 1 4 42 30 0 8 4 7 7 5 3 11 25 2 3
40 1 1 2 1 3 1 1 1 2 3 59 21 3 6 5 4 4 4 3 11 15 2 2
41 2 4 3 4 3 4 2 3 1 3 27 11 1 4 6 7 6 6 1 11 16 4 1
42 1 3 1 3 1 3 1 3 1 3 36 36 5 8 6 4 8 5 3 14 35 2 2
43 3 3 2 3 2 3 2 3 1 2 33 20 0 1 4 9 9 7 0 12 15 5 4
44 4 5 3 5 2 5 1 4 1 1 34 19 0 5 8 8 3 8 2 14 15 6 3
45 5 3 5 3 4 3 2 4 1 1 48 25 0 9 3 6 5 6 7 13 20 2 3
46 4 2 3 2 2 2 2 2 2 2 35 19 0 0 7 6 8 5 6 14 20 5 2
47 2 4 3 4 2 4 2 3 1 3 36 44 2 7 8 9 7 5 2 12 30 4 2
48 3 2 3 1 2 2 1 2 2 3 52 26 0 0 3 6 4 4 2 11 20 4 1
49 2 2 2 2 1 2 1 1 2 3 35 15 2 4 8 7 6 6 1 11 20 3 3
50 6 5 4 5 6 5 1 3 2 1 39 21 0 5 6 9 8 7 8 13 20 4 1
51 1 1 1 1 1 1 1 2 1 4 43 19 3 4 8 9 6 6 1 12 15 4 1
52 1 2 1 2 1 2 1 2 2 3 33 30 3 7 4 4 4 5 3 11 20 2 3
53 2 3 2 3 2 1 2 2 2 4 29 30 0 0 2 7 3 5 1 10 25 4 3
54 5 5 5 5 4 5 3 4 2 1 57 14 0 0 7 9 3 6 3 10 10 4 3
55 1 4 1 4 1 4 1 2 1 3 46 12 2 6 4 8 9 6 2 14 40 5 2
56 1 2 1 2 1 2 2 1 2 3 27 29 3 0 2 6 3 5 4 11 24 4 1
```

Explanation

There are 24 variables. They are as follows:

Variable 1:   subject number

<u>Ratings from 1-5 of craving and difficulty not smoking</u>
Variable 2:   rating of craving for a cigarette after 24 hours'
                abstinence
Variable 3:   rating of difficulty not smoking after 24 hours'
                abstinence
Variable 4:   rating of craving for a cigarette after 48 hours'
                abstinence
Variable 5:   rating of difficulty not smoking after 48 hours'
                abstinence
Variable 6:   rating of craving for a cigarette after 72 hours'
                abstinence
Variable 7:   rating of difficulty not smoking after 72 hours'

	abstinence
Variable 8:	rating of craving for a cigarette after 96 hours' abstinence
Variable 9:	rating of difficulty not smoking after 96 hours' abstinence
Variable 10:	sex 1=female/2=male
Variable 11:	experimental condition 1=nothing, 2=hypnosis, 3=acupuncture, 4=tranquillizers.
Variable 12:	age
Variable 13:	expired-air carbon monoxide concentrations (an index of the amount of cigarette smoke inhaled on the day of measurement)

Scores from 0-9 on smoking motivation measures

Variable 14:	smoking for psycho-social reasons
Variable 15:	smoking for oral gratification
Variable 16:	smoking for pleasurable relaxation
Variable 17:	smoking stimulant effects
Variable 18:	smoking for calming effects
Variable 19:	smoking without thinking about it
Variable 20:	smoking to relieve craving

Variable 21:	smoking dependence score
Variable 22:	cigarettes normally smoked per day
Variable 23:	which of seven possible smoking motives subjects considered the most important for them: 1=social reasons, 2=oral gratification, 3=pleasurable relaxation, 4=stimulation, 5=calming, 6=smoking without thinking about it, 7=to relieve craving
Variable 24:	which of five possible cigarette withdrawal symptoms subjects consider to be most troublesome: 1=poor concentration,

2=irritability, 3=depression, 4=hunger, 5=restlessness

In some cases, you will see 9s or 99s. Some of these are special codes which indicate that this value is missing (probably because the subject failed to provide the necessary information or rating). You should type these numbers in. You will see in Chapter 3 how to tell the computer that they are actually **missing value codes**.

Note: These data are fictitious and have been adapted to provide examples of all the analyses in this book in a single data set.

Index